IN PRAISE OF NUNS

IN PRAISE OF NUNS
An Anthology of Verse

EDITED BY

JAMES M. HAYES

✝

Granger Index Reprint Series

BOOKS FOR LIBRARIES PRESS
PLAINVIEW, NEW YORK

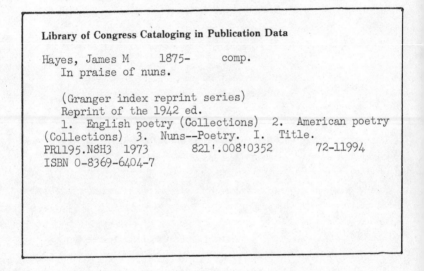

Library of Congress Cataloging in Publication Data

Hayes, James M   1875-   comp.
  In praise of nuns.

  (Granger index reprint series)
  Reprint of the 1942 ed.
  1. English poetry (Collections) 2. American poetry
(Collections) 3. Nuns--Poetry. I. Title.
PR1195.N8H3 1973   821'.008'0352   72-11994
ISBN 0-8369-6404-7

PREFACE

THE word anthology, like other imposing words in our language, comes from the Greeks. It characterizes a collection of verse by various authors and, like the making of books in general, of its making there is no end. On the shelves of every well-stocked library are anthologies of Georgian, Victorian, Catholic, religious, mystical, magazine and newspaper poems. The list is too long for enumeration here, yet we do not find upon it an anthology of poems about the lives of our Catholic sisters, and the holy and useful work they are doing for God's glory and man's welfare.

When Maurice Francis Egan, man of letters and diplomat, returned to America from his post as Minister to Denmark, he suggested that someone make a collection of poems about the holy women of our convents.* As far as is known this is the first attempt to follow Doctor Egan's suggestion, and it is given to the public with the hope that it will be the precursor of an anthology more complete and more satisfactory.

Since the days of Martha—the sister of Mary and Lazarus, and according to a venerable tradition the first Christian to become a nun — our Catholic people have always loved and revered the religious women who, giving themselves to God, bless the world by their prayers and labors. It is no surprise to find in our Catholic poetry many poems of distinction in appreciation of the conventual life.

Because among those who are not members of the household of the Faith, many have misunderstood, and unfavorably and unjustly represented in prose and verse the lives and

* "It is a pity that an anthology of really good poems — there are a great many amateurish ones — can not be made by a discriminating hand, of poems written in honor of *religieuses*, and among the first, should be placed this poem of Father Earls', ('To a Nun Of the Good Shepherd') and Father Hayes' lovely and Appealing 'Old Nuns.' " (Maurice Francis Egan, *America*, June 24, 1922.)

[5]

labors of our sisters, it will give a thrill of joy to every Catholic heart to read the noble and beautiful tributes to them in the verses gathered from the poetry of those who do not profess our Catholic Faith. We are aware that now and then a few strike a note that does not ring true to Catholic ears, but we have included their verses because the occasional note sounds only faintly in the melodies that sing their praise and admiration of our Sisters.

Twenty-five years ago when Joyce Kilmer compiled an anthology of poems he liked best, he gave us no poem by an American nun. Had God spared him to our present day, he could find in convents some of the best poetry of our times. In poems written by sisters of the different communities, he could give us poetry that is admired not only by the children of the Church, but poetry that has won for itself a high place in the literary world. And this is as it should be, for it is the mind of Francis Thompson that in the soil of the Church grow together the palm and the laurel, Dominic and Dante, sanctity and song.* And was it not in the convent of Whitby on its high cliff by the North Sea, and under the patronage of Hilda, saint and nun, that Caedmon wrote our first native English verse?

The selected poems by nuns give us a glimpse of convent life from within. In them we see rays of the sunshine that floods convent cells; in them we hear echoes of Wordsworth's singing words,

"Nuns fret not at their convent's narrow room."

Nuns are happy because all the sacrifices, privations and difficulties of their lives are made bearable by love, the love of the "Tremendous Lover," Jesus, whose brides they have vowed themselves to be in time and for eternity. In the motto that Chaucer gives to his Prioress is the secret of a nun's life,

"Love conquers all things."

* Essay on Shelley.

[6]

ACKNOWLEDGMENTS

The editor and publisher are grateful to the following for permission to use the material listed:

America for "The Little Flower" by Leonard Feeney, S.J.; "Unheeded Vocation" by Eleanore L. Perry; "For a Novice" by Sister Mary Edwardine; "On a Certain Nun" by Sister Mary Ignatia; and "Saint Teresa of Avila" by Sister Mary Saint Virginia.

D. Appleton-Century Co., Inc., for "Perpetual Vows," taken from *Starshine and Candlelight* by Sister Mary Angelita; and "Questions on a Nun's Habit" from *Penelope and Other Poems* by Sister Mary Madeleva, also permission of Sister Mary Madeleva.

Avon House for "To a Nun" by Mary Terry Gill.

Benziger Brothers, publisher and copyright owner, for "To a Nun of the Good Shepherd," from *The Road Beyond the Town and Other Poems* by Rev. Michael Earls, S.J.; "The Soldier and the Nun" and "The World to any Nun" from *Love Folds Its Wings* by Sister Mary Eleanore, C.S.C.; "Mother Mary Xavier" from *Passion Flowers* by Rev. Benjamin Dionysius Hill, C.P., and "The Nun's Vow" from *Cloister Flowers* by Sister Mary Wilfrid de la Motte.

Burns, Oates & Washbourne, England, for "The Teresian Contemplative," taken from *Poems* by Hugh Benson.

Francis Carlin for "The Baby of Saint Brigid."

D. A. Casey for "The Spouse of Christ."

The Catholic World for "A Nun" by J. O. Austin; "The Cloister" by Mother Mary Campion, also permission of

Mother Mary Campion, S.H.C.J.; "Sister Veronica" by Margaret Holmes; and "Victim Invisible" by Sister Miriam.

A. F. Cody and the University of Santa Clara Press for "The Sister of Charity," taken from *Enchanted Casements.*

The Commonweal for "The Convent Garden" by Marie Kirkwood; and "Death of Saint Thérèse of Lisieux" by Jessica Powers, also permission of Jessica Powers.

Dodd Mead & Co., Inc., for "Saint Bride's Lullaby" by Fiona Macleod.

Doubleday, Doran & Co., Inc., for "To Two Little Sisters of the Poor" by Aline Kilmer, taken from *Candles that Burn,* copyright 1927.

John Durkan for "The Sisterhood of God" by Patrick F. Durkan.

Elkin, Mathews and Marrot — London, Eng. for "Cor Cordium" and "The White Sisters of Culion."

Farrar & Rinehart, Inc., for "The Blind Nun" and "Saint Teresa," taken from *The Shadow of the Perfect Rose* by Thomas S. Jones, Jr., copyright 1937 by John L. Foley.

Rev. Edward F. Garesché, S.J., for "The Nuns."

Garden City Publishing Co., Inc., for "The Prioress," taken from J. U. Nicolson's translation of *The Canterbury Tales.*

Harper & Brothers for "Young Nun" from *Radiant Quest* by Grace Noll Crowell; "Epithalamium" from *Earthbound and Other Poems* and "Sister Mary Conceptia" from *Balm in Gilead,* both by Helene Mullins.

Mrs. Jessie Gill Hartman for "Soeur Fidèle" by Frances Gill.

[8]

Houghton Mifflin Company for "Sister Saint Luke" by John Hay; and "The White Veil" by Grace Fallow Norton.

The Irish Monthly for "A Nun's Heart," Anonymous; and "Hide and Seek" by Sister Mary Philip, C.S.C.

P. J. Kennedy & Sons for "To Mother Mary Xavier," taken from *Shepherd My Thoughts* by Francis P. Donnelly, S.J., also permission of the author; and "The Divine Call," taken from *Poems* by Sister Mary Genevieve Todd, also permission of the Sisters of Providence.

Elenita Thompson Kirkpatrick for "Beneath the Sanctuary Lamp."

Longmans, Green & Co., Inc., for "The Day of My Profession" by Sister Mary Christina, taken from *A Daughter of Coventry Patmore, Sister Mary Christina,* S.H.C.J., by a Religious of the Society of the Holy Child Jesus.

Mrs. Denis A. McCarthy for "In the Nuns' Garden," taken from *The Harp of Life* by Denis A. McCarthy.

The Macmillan Company and the authors for "A Nun Speaks to Mary," "A Question of Lovers" and "I Visit Carmel," taken from *Selected Poems* by Sister Mary Madeleva; "A Carmelite Breaks Silence" and "The Tower of Lowliness," taken from *Woven of the Sky* by Sister Miriam; and "Arcum Conteret" and "On a Favorite Poet," taken from *Now There Is Beauty* by Sister Mary Thérèse.

Macmillan & Co., Ltd., London, for "The Convent Garden," taken from *Collected Poems* by Katherine Tynan Hinkson.

Francis Maguire for "Quaint Rider."

The Magnificat and the authors for "God's Handmaid" by

Rev. Hugh F. Blunt; "Ideal" by Sister Miriam Clare, O.S.F.; "Vocation" by Sister Mary David, O.M.; "To a Nun Violinist" by Sister Mary Louise; "The Nun" by Shiel MacDara; "In the Larger Novitiate" by Catharine McPartlin; "To a Nun Decorated with the Iron Cross" by J. Corson Miller; "Resignation" by Julia Claire O'Connor; and "To My Nun Sister" by Rev. E. P. Tirvan, S.J.

Mother Mary Rose Huber, O.S.D., for "Impress of the Crucifix" by Mother Alphonsa, O.S.D.

Benjamin Francis Musser for "A Fire Shall Burn Before Him" and "Elderly Nun."

The Nation for "A Little Nun" by Edith Loomis.

A. Page, C.S.A. (Gerald M. C. Fitzgerald), for "A Sister" and "Sister and Nun."

The Pilot Publishing Company for "Vanquished" by Katherine E. Conway, taken from *On the Sunrise Slope*.

Poetry and the author for "A Lonely Flute" by Odell Shepard.

Jessica Powers for "Death In Carmel" and "Death of Saint Thérèse of Lisieux."

St. Anthony's Guild and the authors for "A Nun's Diamond Jubilee," taken from *The Golden Flame and Other Verse* by Gertrude Jane Codd; and "Exchange" by Sister Mary Dorothy Ann, taken from *Songs of the Rood*.

Sands & Company, London, and the author for "A Ditty of Saint Clare" by Enid Dinnis.

Charles Scribner's Sons for "Soeur Monique" by Alice Meynell.

Sister Mary Angeline, S.S.N.D., for "Laughter in Heaven."

Sister Mary Colman, S.S.N.D., for "Prayer for a Silver Jubilee."

Sister Mary Eugene, S.S.N.D., for "Convent Morning" and "Maureen O'Reilly."

Sister Margaret Maria for "Martyrs of Nazareth."

Sister Monica for "The Reply," also permission of *The Placidian;* and "The Teacher," also permission of *The Commonweal.*

Sister Mary Thérèse, Sor.D.S., for "Christmas in Carmel," "Port-of-Call," and "To a Nun-Stigmatist."

Sister Maris Stella for "In Memory of Mother Seraphine Ireland."

Sister Mary of the Angels, R.S.M., for "A Nun's Hobby."

The Sisters of Notre Dame de Namur for "Sister Anna Raphael, S.N.D." by E. Mary.

Spirit for "Letter from a Postulant" by Sister Mary Irma, B.V.M.; "A Sister Lights the Candles" by Sister Mary Jeremy, O.P., also permission of the author; and "Profession Song" by Sister Mary of the Visitation.

John Stigall for "A Beggar for God."

Nancy Byrd Turner for "Sister Mary Veronica."

CONTENTS

I

Tributes From Catholic Poets

II

TRIBUTES FROM POETS WHO ARE NOT CATHOLIC

III

POEMS BY NUNS ABOUT NUNS

I

TRIBUTES FROM CATHOLIC POETS

A NUN

J. O. Austin

That I to God, unfettered, may aspire,
And from all lesser loves my spirit wean,
Let my young heart, in solitude serene,
Retain its deep virginity entire:

Let sight of peaks girt with the splendid fire
Of setting suns, or topped by cloudless sheen,
Be barred from me; Let music henceforth mean
Only the chanting of a convent choir.

And if I must be purified of stain
By anguish, free me, God, from every chill
Or tremor at my torment, for I fain
Would bow to Thee a consecrated will,
And brave, with Christ, the darkest depths of pain
To quell desire, unselfish love to gain.

SAINT WINEFRIDE*

C. W. Barraud, S.J.

Blessed Saint Winefride, at thy fair shrine
　　Still to the hard-hearted people of thine
　　　God His ineffable mercy unveils,
Healing the halt and the blind and the dumb —
　　All who for love of Saint Winefride come;
　　　Gentle Saint Winefride, Flower of Wales.

Glorious Alban, first fruit of our seed,
　　Cuthbert, and Dunstan and Wilfrid and Bede,
　　　Thomas, our martyr, who fought the good fight,
Edward, our King, and a thousand saints more,
　　Plead for poor England; but not as of yore
　　　Showing their splendor; for oh! it is night.

What a joy, then, O Maiden is thine,
　　Chosen by God on our darkness to shine,
　　　Chosen to comfort, to soothe, to uplift!
As, when the merle hath forgotten his song,
　　Through the wild winter so dreary, so long,
　　　Pipeth the robin upon the snow-drift.

---

* Saint Winefride was an Abbess in Wales. She was a niece of Saint Bueno who, when leaving Holywell, promised in the name of God that to whomever at the well would ask for a grace through the intercession of Saint Winefride, it would be granted. All through the ages since then, and even when England had repudiated the doctrine of the intercession of saints, many from England and Wales have visited Saint Winefride's well to obtain graces for soul and body.

Editor

[16]

Taller the lily and sweeter the rose,
   Brighter full many a flower that blows
      In the gay summer-time: yet we love best
That little blossom that taketh its birth
   From the cold heart of the snow-covered earth,
      Emblem of love with deep sorrow oppressed.

Emblem of hope in a joy that shall be,
   Emblem of maidenhood, emblem of thee,
      Maiden and martyr! Then bid us arise.
Winter is passing and spring near at hand
   Bringing the sun, the warm sun to our land,
      Leaves to the forest and light to the skies.

Winefride, Winefride, gentle and kind!
   Heal the dull ears and the eyes that are blind.
      If, as thy fountain, thy love never fails,
Flood the whole land with thy mercies and show
   God is not far from us, e'en in our woe,
      Winefride, Winefride, Flower of Wales!

THE TERESIAN CONTEMPLATIVE

Robert Hugh Benson

She moves in tumult; round her lies
   The silence of the world of grace;
The twilight of our mysteries
   Shines like high noonday on her face.
Our piteous guesses, dim with fears,
She touches, handles, sees, and hears.

In her all longings mix and meet;
   Dumb souls through her are eloquent;
She feels the world beneath her feet
   Thrill in a passionate intent:
Through her our tides of feeling roll
And find their God within her soul.

Her faith — the awful Face of God
   Brightens and blinds with utter light;
Her footsteps fall where late He trod;
   She sinks in roaring voids of night;
Cries to her Lord in black despair,
And knows, yet knows not, He is there.

A willing sacrifice she takes
   The burden of our fall within;
Holy she stands; while on her breaks
   The lightning of the wrath of sin;
She drinks her Savior's cup of pain,
And, one with Jesus, thirsts again.

GOD'S HANDMAID
*For a Sister's Jubilee**

HUGH F. BLUNT, LL.D

There was a gentle Maiden,
So many years ago;
With joy her heart was laden,
For God had loved her so.

* Father Blunt wrote this poem for the Silver Jubilee of Sister Mary Ignatia of the Manchester Sisters of Mercy. Thirty-four years ago she established, and through all these long years has ably edited, *The Magnificat* whose devotional and literary value makes it one of our better class Catholic monthlies. As Sister Mary Ignatia is above all a Sister of Mercy, she is true to her vocation, "the service of the poor, the sick, and the ignorant." In the citation read at Boston College of the Society of Jesus when Cardinal O'Connell conferred upon her the honorary degree of Doctor of Laws, among other things it was said "To aid her in the work of the *Magnificat*, Sister Mary Ignatia enlisted the services of girls more blessed with talent than with the gifts of fortune. In the 'Magnificat Home' they received the opportunity of a superior education amid appropriate surroundings, and at the same time found the means of developing their personal gifts. From this in time grew the 'Magnificat Art Company' an institution combining the fine and practical arts. Then followed 'Our Lady of Grace Home' where invalids are not only cared for but also are enabled to become self-supporting through their own activities which are often of genuine creative value. Next came the founding of 'Our Lady of Grace School' affiliated with the Catholic University in Washington, where young women in straitened circumstances are aided in fitting themselves for professional careers, some of them attaining the status of College professors. Lastly was established 'St. Philomena's Home' another institution for the handicapped — one magazine, and five institutions of education and charity are witnesses to what the zeal and piety of one valiant woman can accomplish.—"

We add that she is truly a worthy daughter of the saintly founder of her order, Mary Catherine McAuley.—

Editor

[19]

She craved nor wealth nor power
From Him her heart adored;
She asked this only dower —
A handmaid of her Lord.

O glad annunciation
Of Holy Gabriel;
With her of lowly station
The Godhead comes to dwell.
For He hath now regarded
Her sweet humility,
And with Himself rewarded
Her who His slave would be.

     ✿   ✿   ✿   ✿

There was another maiden —
(That maid was you I'd say)
Whose hands with gifts were laden
For God, one Lady Day.
To serve as handmaid lowly,
The only boon you craved;
Ah, gift to Him most Holy —
To be to Him enslaved!

And now this morning holy
Again comes Gabriel,
To seek you, maiden lowly,
God's word to you to tell.
Ah, list the angel singing
God's hymn of love so true —
"This gift of love I'm bringing —
My Heart — handmaid, to you."

THE BABY OF SAINT BRIGID
(*The First Irish Nun*)

Francis Carlin

Since first the beams of Summer lit
The world to gladden the Infinite,
No maiden walked in Erin fair
Like good Saint Brigid of green Kildare.

For there was more in the eyes of her
Than human light, and her tresses were
As the beams that dance on an Easter morn,
When the Life of the World from Death is born.

Upon a day as Brigid prays
In an ecstasy, a Babe was laid
On her open arms by Angels three,
Who stood to guard the mystery.

Now being wise in Faith she knew
The little Child to be the Jew
Whom Patrick called the living God,
The Native-Born of every sod.

And being wise in hope she kissed
The dimples in her Darling's fist.
And being wise in love she sung
A lullaby in her ancient tongue.

Then the angels guarding the mystery
Of a sleeping Babe on a maiden's knee,
Bent low to her in whispering joy;
"Hail! Foster-mother of Mary's Boy!"

"Since you have sung Him into sleep
We promise for to come and peep
Into the dream of every child,
By Erinn's slumber-song beguiled."

And even yet in Ireland
The slumbering babe with dimpled hands
Would clutch the dreams where Angels peep
Since Brigid sang her Babe to sleep.

THE SPOUSE OF CHRIST

D. A. CASEY

He came from out eternal years,
A smile upon his lips, a tender smile
That, somehow, spoke of partings and of tears.

'Twas eventide and silence brooded low
On earth and sky — the hour when haunting fears
Of mystery pursue us as we go.

Strange, mystic shadows filled the temple dim,
But on the Golden Door the ruby glow
Spoke orisons more sweet than vesper hymn.

No human accents voiced His gentle call,
No crashing thunderbolts did wait on Him
As when of old He deigned to summon Saul.

But heart did speak to heart, an unseen chord
In Love's own scale did sweetly rise and fall:
Nor questioned she, but meekly answered "Lord!"

To-night some household counts a vacant chair,
But far on high Christ portions the reward
A hundredfold for each poor human care.

THE PRIORESS

Geoffrey Chaucer

But to say something of her moral sense,
She was so charitable and piteous
That she would weep if she but saw a mouse
Caught in a trap, though it were dead or bled.
She had some little dogs, too, which she fed
On roasted flesh, or milk and fine white bread.
But sore she'd weep if one of them were dead,
Or if men smote it with a rod to smart:
For pity ruled her and her tender heart.
Right decorous her pleated wimple was;
Her nose was fine, her eyes as blue as glass;
Her mouth was small and therewith soft and red;
But certainly she had a fair forehead,
It was almost a full span broad, I own,
For, truth to tell, she was not undergrown.
Neat was her cloak, as I was well aware.
Of coral small, about her arm she'd bear
A string of beads and gauded all with green;
And therefrom hung a brooch of golden sheen
Whereon was first written a crownéd "A",
And under *Amor vincit omnia.*

A NUN'S DIAMOND JUBILEE

GERTRUDE JANE CODD

When we remember that dear childhood day
That brought us first within the convent door,
And that next memory cherished even more ——
The chapel, and the Cardinal, in May,
And that first kiss of God; and then the way
We grew to womanhood and learned the lore
That comes from books and love and heaven's store:
There are a thousand words that we might say.

Oh, roses that have bloomed through all the years,
Oh, garden paths and iris by the wall,
Whose image do you bring us all the while?
Dear one who loved us, taught us, dried our tears,
May God's sweet benediction on you fall,
And give us still the blessing of your smile.

THE SISTER OF CHARITY

Alexander J. Cody, S.J.

She hastens through the dingy street;
Where'er she goes is God's retreat;
Where'er she tarries lingers grace,
The sunshine of her Savior's face.

Her cell, no monastery brick,
But some drab bed-room of the sick;
Her chapel, rich in love's desire,
Some vacant pew 'neath parish spire:

Her grill, a virgin's holy fear —
The Bridegroom ever walketh near;
Her veil, our Lady's modesty
That hungering angels yearn to see.

She hastens through the dingy street;
Where'er she goes is God's retreat;
Where'er she tarries lingers grace,
The sunshine of her Savior's face.

VANQUISHED
(*For A Nun's Profession*)

KATHERINE E. CONWAY

Yea, vanquished am I — thralled at last and bound!
Vain, vain to strive against the Strong — all vain
The toil, the tears, the weariness, the drain
Of hot heart's blood from many a cruel wound —
Lost, lost for Earth and Heaven! But lo! I've found —
I a veiled captive in His triumph train,
Joy that effaceth memory of pain.
"Thy days," the world said, "run in dreary round;
Naught hast thou gained, but much hath forfeited.
Art thou not fain — speak true! — again to be
Unfettered on the flower — strewn pathway broad?"
"Ah, tighten these dear bonds," I shuddering said —
"My Conqueror, but not mine Enemy,
Nay, but my Friend of friends, my King, my God!"

A HYMN IN HONOR OF SAINT TERESA, A CARMELITE NUN

Richard Crashaw

Love, thou art Absolute sole lord
Of life and death. To prove the word
We'll now appeal to none of all
Those thy old soldiers, great and tall,
Ripe men of martyrdom, that could reach down
With strong arms, their triumphant crown;
Such as could with lusty breath
Speak loud into the face of death
Their great Lord's glorious name, to none
Of those whose spacious bosoms spread a throne
For Love at large to fill, spare blood and sweat;
And see him take a private seat,
Making his mansion in the mild
And milky soul of a soft child.

   Scarce had she learned to lisp the name
Of Martyr; yet she thinks it shame
Life should so long play with that breath
Which spent could buy so brave a death.
She never undertook to know
What death with love, should have to do;
Nor has she e'er yet understood
Why to shew love, she should shed blood.
Yet though she can not tell you why,
She can love and she can die.

   Scarce had she blood enough to make
A guilty sword blush for her sake;
Yet has she a Heart dares hope to prove
How much less strong is death than love.

Be love but there; let poor six years
Be pos'd with the maturest fears
Man trembles at, you straight shall find
Love knows no nonage, nor the mind.
'Tis Love, not years nor limbs that can
Make the Martyr or the man.

Love toucht her Heart, and lo it beats
High, and burns with such brave heats;
Such thirsts to die, so dares drink up
A thousand cold deaths in one cup.
Good reason. For she breathes all fire.
Her weak breast heaves with strong desire
Of what she may with fruitless wishes
Seek from amongst her mother's kisses.

Since 'tis not to be had at home
She'll travel to a Martyrdom.
No home for her confesses she
But where she may a Martyr be.

She'll to the Moors: and trade with them,
For this unvalued Diadem.
She'll offer them her dearest breath,
With Christ's Name in't in change for death.
She'll bargain with them; and will give
Them God; teach them how to live
In Him: or, if they this deny,
For Him she'll teach them how to die.
So shall she leave amongst them sown
Her Lord's blood; or at least her own.

Farewell then, all the world! Adieu.
Teresa is no more for you.
Farewell pleasures, sports and joys,
(Never till now esteemed toys)
Farewell whatever dear may be

Mother's arms or Father's knee.
Farewell house and farewell home!
She's for the Moors and Martyrdom.
    Sweet, not so fast! lo thy fair Spouse
Whom thou seekest with so swift vows,
Calls thee back, and bids thee come
To embrace a milder martyrdom.
    Blest powers forbid, Thy tender life
Should bleed upon a barbarous knife;
Or some base hand have power to race
Thy breast's chaste cabinet, or uncase
A soul kept there so sweet, oh no;
Wise heav'n will never have it so.
Thou art love's victim; and must die
A death more mystical and high.
Into Love's arms thou shalt let fall
A still-surviving funeral.
His is the Dart must make the Death
Whose stroke shall taste thy hallow'd breath;
A Dart thrice dipped in that rich Flame
Which writes thy Spouse's radiant Name
Upon the roof of Heav'n; where aye
It shines and with a sovereign ray
Beats bright upon the burning faces
Of souls which in that Name's sweet graces
Finds everlasting smiles. So rare
So spiritual, pure and fair
Must be th' immortal instrument
Upon whose choice point shall be sent
A life so lov'd; And that there be
Fit executioners for thee,
The fairest and first-born sons of fire
Blest Seraphim, shall leave their choir

And turn love's soldiers upon thee
To exercise their archery.
   O how oft shall thou complain
Of a sweet and subtle pain.
Of intolerable joys;
Of a Death, in which who dies
Loves his death and dies again,
And would forever so be slain,
And lives and dies; and know not why
To live, But that he thus may never leave to die.
   How kindly will thy gentle Heart
Kiss the sweetly killing Dart!
And close in his embraces keep
Those delicious Wounds, that weep
Balsam to heal themselves with. Thus
When these thy Deaths, so numerous
Shall all at once die into one,
And melt thy soul's sweet mansion;
Like a soft lump of incense, hasted
By too hot fire, and wasted
Into perfuming clouds, so fast
Shalt thou exhale to Heav'n at last
In a resolving sigh, and then
O what? Ask not the tongues of men.
Angels cannot tell, suffice
Thyself shall feel thy own full joys
And hold them fast forever there.
So soon as you first appear,
The Moon of maiden stars, thy white
Mistress, attended by such bright
Souls as thy shining self, shall come
And in her first ranks make thee room;
Where 'mongst her snowy family

Immortal welcomes wait for thee.

O what delight, when reveal'd Life shall stand
And teach thy lips heav'n with his hand;
On which thou now may'st to thy wishes
Heap up thy consecrated kisses.
What joys shall seize thy soul, when she
Bending her blessed eyes on thee
(Those second smiles of Heav'n) shall dart
Her mild rays through thy melting heart!

Angels, thy old friends, there shall greet thee
Glad at their own home now to greet thee.

All thy good Works which went before
And waited for thee at the door,
Shall own thee there; and all in one
Weave thee a constellation
Of Crowns, with which the King thy Spouse
Shall build up thy triumphant brows.

All thy old woes shall now smile on thee
And thy pains sit bright upon thee
All thy suff'rings be divine.
Tears shall take comfort, and turn gems
And wrongs repent to diadems.
Even thy Death shall live; and new
Dress the soul that erst they slew.
Thy wounds shall blush to such bright scars
As keep account of the Lamb's wars.

Those rare Works where thou shalt leave writ
Love's noble history, with wit

Taught thee by none but him, while here
They feed our souls, shall clothe thine there.
Each heav'nly word by whose hid flame
Our hard hearts shall strike fire, the same
Shall flourish on thy brows, and be

Both fire to us, and flame to thee;
Whose light shall live bright in thy face
By glory, in our hearts by grace.
    Thou shalt look round about, and see
Thousands of crown'd souls flock to be
Themselves thy crown. Sons of thy vows
The virgin-births, with which thy sovereign Spouse
Made fruitful thy fair soul, go now
And with them all about thee bow
To him; Put on, He'll say, put on
(My rosy love) that thy rich zone
Sparkling with the sacred flames
Of thousand souls, whose happy names
Heav'n kept upon thy score (Thy bright
Life brought them first to kiss the light
That kindled them to stars.) and so
Thou with the Lamb, thy Lord, shalt go;
And wheresoe'r He sets His white
Steps, walk with Him those ways of light
Which who in death would live to see
Must learn in life to die like thee.

DESCRIPTION OF A CONVENT

Richard Crashaw

No roofs of gold o'er riotous tables shining,
Whole days and suns devoured with endless dining;
No sails of Tyrian silk, proud pavements sweeping,
Nor ivory couches, costlier slumbers keeping:
Our lodgings hard and homely as our fare,
That chaste and cheap, as the few clothes we wear;
A hasty portion of prescribéd sleep;
Obedient slumbers that can wake and weep;
And work for work, not wages: let to-morrow's
New drops wash of the sweat of this day's sorrow:
A long and daily dying life, which breathes
A respiration of reviving deaths.
But neither are there those ignoble stings
That nip the bosom of the world's best things:
No cruel guard of diligent cares, that keep
Crowned woes awake, as things too wise for sleep:
But reverend discipline, and religious fear,
And soft obedience, find sweet biding here:
Silence and sacred rest, peace and pure joys;
And room enough for monarchs, while none swells
Beyond the kingdom of contented cells.

THE FLAMING HEART
To Saint Teresa

RICHARD CRASHAW

Leave her that; and thou shalt leave her
Not one loose shaft but love's whole quiver.
For in love's field was never found
A nobler weapon than a wound.
Love's passives are his activ'st parts,
The wounded is the wounding heart.
O Heart! the equal poise of love's both parts
Big alike with wounds and darts.
Live in these conquering leaves; live all the same;
And walk through all tongues one triumphant Flame.
Live here, great Heart; and love and die and kill;
And bleed and wound; and yield and conquer still.
Let this immortal life where'er it comes
Walk in a crowd of loves and martyrdoms.
Let mystic Deaths wait on't; and wise souls be
The love-slain witnesses of this life of thee.
Oh sweet incendiary! Shew here thy art,
Upon the carcass of a hard, cold heart,
Let all the scatter'd shafts of light, that play
Among the leaves of thy large Books of day,
Combin'd against this Breast at once break in
And take away from me myself and sin,
This gracious Robbery shall thy bounty be;
And my best fortunes such fair spoils of me.
Oh thou undaunted daughter of desires!
By all thy dow'r of Lights and Fires;
By all the eagle in thee, all the dove;
By all thy lives and deaths of love;

By thy large draughts of intellectual day,
And by thy thirst of love more large than they;
By all thy brim-filled Bowles of fierce desire,
By thy last morning's draught of liquid fire;
By the full kingdom of that final kiss
That seized thy parting Soul, and seal'd thee his;
By all the heav'ns thou hast in him
(Fair sister of the Seraphim!)
By all of Him we have in Thee;
Leave nothing of myself in me.
Let me so read thy life that I
Unto all life of mine may die.

SAINT FRIDESWIDA*
An Anglo-Saxon Nun

AUBREY DE VERE

One love I; One: within His bridal bower
My feet shall tread: One love I, One alone:
His mother is a Virgin, and His Sire
The unfathomed fount of pureness undefiled:
Him love I Whom to love is to be chaste:
Him love I touched by Whom my forehead shines:
Whom she that clasps grows spotless more and more:
Behold, to mine His Spirit He hath joined:
And His the blood that mantles in my cheek:
His ring is on my finger.

* It was revealed to Saint Frideswida that in that place near the Isis where she had opened a blind man's eyes, and healed a leper, God would one day raise up a seat of learning, the light and health of the realm (The University of Oxford).

Editor

MONASTICISM

Aubrey De Vere

The spirit has its passion as the sense:
A spiritual ear there is, a spiritual eye,
A spiritual heart whose "fires of light" supply
To earthly heart love's true intelligence:
And answering these, beyond thy narrow fence,
O Nature, spreads, remotest yet most nigh,
That spiritual universe of Deity
Wherein alone creation lives and whence.

Behold the things that are! 'Tis we, alas,
That shadow-charmed, and drowned in things
    that seem,
Live without hope and die without a sign:
Alone the life monastic spurns the dream,
Crying to all the ages as they pass,
"The strongest of man's love is love Divine."

A DITTY OF SAINT CLARE

Enid Dinnis

The holy Lady Poverty
Looked on the Lady Clare,
In silken garb arrayed was she —
With gems adorned, how meagerly —
And longed to make her fair.

And longed of her a queen to make,
A queen of Mary's line;
Clad even as the lilies are,
A brighter thing than Bethlehem's star,
On darksome night to shine.

Came Francis, her ambassador,
From goodly realms of dearth;
A story of the Lord he told
Whose wealth you may not count in gold,
A mighty man of mirth —

Told of the wonderland of Christ,
Where all that's last is first,
Until the heart of Clare was rent
By God's most holy discontent.
Oh, blest are they that thirst!

Till rose she from her father's halls
A goodlier work to seek —
Rose up by violence to take,
A doughty dame for Jesu's sake,
The kingdom of the meek.

[39]

So with the Lady Poverty
The rugged road she trod,
Who, fearless, chose the better part.
Oh, blessed are the pure in heart
For they shall look on God!

She saw a sacramental sky
And Heaven-reflecting sea;
And lo! in every living thing
A fellow-servant of the King
Who walked in Galilee.

She saw the hills in rapture held,
Immutable in prayer;
She shared the valley's mystic dream,
And heard the vespers of the stream,
The beggar-maid, Saint Clare.

So rough-clad in her native cell
She lived, by sorrow tried,
Nor mourned, save that the mourner blest
Is comforted at Jesu's breast:
So lived Saint Clare and died.

And still in holy Church to-day
In lives of love and prayer
They tell the story of the three —
The holy Lady Poverty,
Saint Francis and Saint Clare.

SISTER MARY ALPHONSA*

Eleanor C. Donnelly

They made her a grave where the tall grasses wave
  'Neath the blue of the Western sky,
And they laid her to sleep where the wild waves sweep,
  Through the bending reeds that sigh.

With many a prayer they laid her there,
  To sleep in that cold, cold bed,
While on her bier fell as holy a tear
  As ever embalmed the dead.

O bride of the Lamb, thou hast gone home!
  In the Virgin's train art thou;
And the songs that rise o'er the dome of the skies
  But echo thy virgin vow.

Let fancy bright, on the wings of light
  Now seek that lonely grave,
Where flowers bloom and the wild birds sing
  By the dark Arkansas wave.

May no ruder wind sweep across thy sleep
  Than the breath of summer roses,
While virtue's tear embalms the bier
  Where our martyred dead reposes.

---

* Sister Mary Alphonsa was a Sister of Loretto of Kentucky who died on her way to Santa Fe in 1867. Bishop Lamy wrote; "The youngest Sister of Loretto died, on the 24th of July, from fright, as I considered it, caused by the attack of the savages. She was eighteen years old, well educated and a model of virtue." Bishop Lamy was the first bishop and later the first archbishop of Santa Fe. He is the hero of Willa Cather's popular novel, *Death Comes for the Archbishop*.

Editor

MOTHER MARY XAVIER*

Francis P. Donnelly, S.J.

Bless with the splendor white of God's new shrine
   Your golden years of half a century:
   And, Mother, for past days and days to be
Let love fulfilled, and promised love entwine
In praise and pledges, while the vestal line
   Of blessing priests and cloistered charity
   Fill with the grateful voice of jubilee
The hallowed arches and the spires divine.

Hark! Echoes answer from an ampler dome
   Where healed and fed and taught, and child hearts — cry
   Their joyous thanks for all your toil and tears:
Temple of charity, God's earth-wide home,
Whose base is everywhere, whose roof the sky,
   Whose sacrifice you are these fifty years.

* Mother Xavier was the founder and for more than fifty years the superior of the Sisters of Charity, Convent Station, New Jersey. The dedication of Saint Elizabeth's College Chapel at Convent Station marked her Golden Jubilee.

Author's Note

NUNS OF THE PERPETUAL ADORATION

Ernest Dowson

Calm, sad, secure; behind high convent walls,
  These watch the sacred lamp, these watch and pray:
And it is one with them when evening falls,
  And one with them the cold return of day.

These heed not time; their days and nights they make
  Into a long returning rosary,
Whereon their lives are threaded for Christ's sake;
  Meekness and vigilance and chastity.

A vowed patrol, in silent companies,
  Life-long they keep before the living Christ.
In the dim church, their prayers and penances
  Are fragrant incense to the Sacrificed.

Outside, the world is wild and passionate;
  Man's weary laughter and his sick despair
Entreat at their impenetrable gate:
  They heed no voices in their dream of prayer.

They saw the glory of the world displayed;
  They saw the bitter of it, and the sweet;
They knew the roses of the world should fade,
  And be trod under by the hurrying feet.

Therefore they rather put away desire,
  And crossed their hands and came to sanctuary,
And veiled their heads and put on coarse attire:
  Because their comeliness was vanity.

And there they rest; they have serene insight
   Of the illuminating dawn to be:
Mary's sweet Star dispels for them the night,
   The proper darkness of humanity.

Calm, sad, secure; with faces worn and mild:
   Surely their choice of vision is the best;
Yea! for our roses fade, the world is wild;
   And there, beside the altar, there is rest.

THE SISTERHOOD OF GOD

Patrick F. Durkan

They are gathered in the cloister, highest type of womankind,
Who have left the world's allurements and its noisy scenes
    behind.
There, their solemn vows are plighted to the Trinity on high,
There they live like choirs angelic, there in sanctity they die.

What is wealth to that meek sister who within her quiet cell
Sees but Him who spoke prophetic to the woman at the well?
What to her is fame whose chaplet is a rosary of tears,
Who has drunk from God's own chalice through a litany of
    years?

Oft beneath that simple habit all the graces are enshrined,
Music, painting, song and science in their varied lights com-
    bined:
For from halls of highest culture went they to the cloister's
    shade,
Who now worship at the altar where their precious gifts are
    laid.

Teach they little ones the lessons that but love can inculcate,
Store their youthful minds with knowledge that befits the
    highest state,
Show they others, by example, how to conquer and to subdue
All of earth, in human longings, all of pride and folly too.

Go they forth to works of mercy counselled by the Son of Man,
Pouring balm upon the wayside like the Good Samaritan,

Seek they where beside a pallet sits a fond and faithful wife
Watching, weeping, hoping, praying for a dear devoted life

Care they for the poor and homeless, old and weak with them
    abide,
Gather they to light and shelter whom the world had cast
    aside,
Calm they troubled hearts and weary when the hour of death
    is near,
Guide they to the gates of Heaven, souls repentant and
    sincere.

Leave they footprints on the desert, live they by the Ganges'
    side,
Sing they where the Orinoco bears its commerce to the tide,
Lift they souls in adoration where the Child and Mary dwelt,
Kneel they too in supplication where the Man of Sorrows
    knelt.

Stand they where the sick and wounded from the battlefield
    have come,
Pale and bleeding, lacerated by the canister and bomb,
Breathe they words of hope and comfort as they smoothe the
    fevered brow,
In the light of love and mercy, they are more than mortals
    now.

Shrink they not from where the leper wears his blighted life
    away,
Dread they not the clime of danger where idolatry holds
    sway.
What is death to them, the plighted, in the service of the Lord
Whether life on earth is ended by disease or by the sword?

Love and praise and benediction win they from the old and
     young,
Art has typified their labors, poets have their glory sung;
Wreaths are theirs, enshrined in Heaven, like the bloom on
     Aaron's rod,
Patient, humble, kind and gentle are the Sisterhood of God.

TO A NUN OF THE GOOD SHEPHERD

Michael Earls, S.J.

If in a wildwood where no sunbeam falls,
Ferocious with the lure of deadly ground,
Some wayward child were lost, with dread inwound,
Afar from safe estate in sheltered walls.
O, praise the man, whom gentle pity calls;
Who dares the wood and monster death around:
Away from death he lifts the child; resound
Again glad voices in a father's halls.

This life is thine: no single sacrifice
Thy silver years proclaim, but numberless;
And numberless the silver praises now
That speak in grateful hearts and tearful eyes;
Poor be their utterance, but rich they bless —
With more than silver does their love endow.

THE LITTLE FLOWER
(*A Carmelite Nun*)

LEONARD FEENEY, S.J.

Knowing that it would burn she courted fire;
And who would wish to chide her heart's desire?

For when the little altar-rose was sweet
And withering beside the candle heat,
And when she saw a beautiful white moth —
Its wings drop flaming to the altar cloth:

Long did she ponder would it not be right
To brave the pain if she could reach the light,
And be Love's fuel as a moth, a rose,
And fall where all earth's bitter beauty goes.

For beauty runneth out as quick as sun,
Quick as a nun lights candles, one by one
For Vespers; swift as swallow-shadows pass
Or field mice trickle through the flowing grass.

Alas for all the violet petals shed
And all last Summer's lilies that are dead! —
For hollyhocks, laburnum, marygold
And whatsoever names the flowers hold!

She heard the bells above the convent chime;
She dreamt of the eternal seeding time
When starry soil, and loam of azure field
Would be her substance and her colors yield.

And so the flame became her heart's desire
Knowing that it would burn she courted fire —
She who had seen upon the altar cloth
The rose's dust, the ashes of a moth.

IN THE CLOISTER

WILLIAM J. FISCHER

She spends her life, far from the noisy mart
  Of commerce, and deep, sunny, azure skies
  Paint all the brighter to her human eyes,
The vales of Solitude, dear to her heart!
And there she toils unknown and bears her part
  Of Life's Gethsemene. Yet, O, the prize!
  Sweet rose-crowned ways lead not to Paradise —
She chose the thorny ways that pain and smart.
A mystic Hand has tuned her fond heart-strings
  To one long hymn of praise, with joy replete,
That fills with music, paths angels have trod
  And from her soul, Love daily, gladly flings
Pearls of prayer — keys that unlock in dire need,
  The audience chamber of the very God.

THE NUNS

EDWARD F. GARESCHÉ, S.J.

I desire
Words that are as sweet as dawn and strong as fire!
I here beseech
From the Immortal Love, felicities of speech;
And thou, serene, celestial maid,
Who art the Mother of God's very Son,
Upon my lips be thy bright fingers laid
Else what I yearn to sing may never be begun!
For joyfully, I see
All sweetest song hath still its source in thee!

For I would praise the virgins of the Lord —
A theme illusive as the lilies are,
Or the swift gleams from sudden sunrise poured,
Or silvery trembling of a timid star.
Yet is much loveliness and majesty
Hid in their lives. So Mary prosper me!

THE SISTER OF CHARITY

Gerald Griffin

She once was a lady of honor and wealth,
Bright glowed in her features the roses of health;
Her vesture was blended of silk and of gold
And her motion shook perfume from every fold:
Joy revelled around her — love shone at her side,
And bright was her smile at the thought of a bride;
But light was her step in the high-sounding hall,
When she heard of the daughters of Vincent de Paul.

She felt in her spirit the summons of grace,
That called her to live for her suffering race;
And heedless of pleasure, of comfort, of home,
Rose quickly like Mary and answered, "I'll come!"
She put from her person the trappings of pride,
And passed from her home, with the joy of a bride;
Nor wept on the threshold, as onward she moved,
For her heart was on fire, in the cause it approved.

Lost ever to fashion — to vanity lost,
That beauty that once was the song and the toast;
No more in the ball-room that figure we meet,
But gliding at dusk to the wretch's retreat.
Forgot in the halls is that high-sounding name,
For the Sister of Charity blushes at fame;
Forgot are the claims of her riches and birth,
For she barters for heaven, the glory of earth.

Those feet that to music could gracefully move,
Now bear her alone on the mission of love;

Those hands that once dangled the perfume and gem,
Are tending the helpless or lifted for them;
That voice that once echoed the song of the vain,
Now whispers relief to the bosom of pain;
And the hair that was shining with diamond and pearl,
Is wet with the tears of the penitent girl.

Her down bed a pallet — her trinkets a bead,
Her lustre — one taper that serves her to read;
Her sculpture — the crucifix nailed by her bed,
Her paintings — one print of the thorn-crownéd head;
Her cushion — the pavement that wearies her knees,
Her music — the psalm, or the sigh of disease:
The delicate lady lives mortified there,
And the feast is forsaken for fasting and prayer.

Yet not to the service of heart or of mind,
Are the cares of that heaven-minded virgin confined;
Like Him Whom she loves to the mansions of grief,
She hastes with the tidings of joy or relief.
She strengthens the weary — she comforts the weak,
And soft is her voice in the ear of the sick;
Where want and affliction on mortals attend,
The Sister of Charity there is a friend.

Unshrinking where pestilence scatters its breath,
Like an angel she moves, 'mid the vapor of death;
Where rings the loud musket, and flashes the sword,
Unfearing she walks, for she follows the Lord.
How sweetly she bends o'er each plague-tainted face
With looks that are lighted with holiest grace;
How kindly she dresses each suffering limb,
For she sees in the wounded the image of Him.

Behold her, ye worldly! behold her, ye vain!
Who shrink from the pathway of virtue and pain;
Who yield up to pleasure your nights and your days,
Forgetful of service, forgetful of praise.
Ye lazy philosophers — self-seeking men —
Ye fireside philanthropists, great at the pen,
How stand in the balance your eloquence weighed
With the life and the deeds of that high-born maid?

A BLEEDING HEART AFLAME.
(*For Saint Margaret Mary, A Visitation Nun*)

JAMES M. HAYES

I longed for joy and peace and deep content,
For life all golden and untouched by tears,
For life unshadowed by the cares and the fears
That fret the heart, for life of high intent.
    Alas, the shadows lengthen and my days are spent,
    With weary feet I tread the barren years.

Some hold that love is all that life requires,
Love fills the heart and makes the spirit glad:
Much love was mine and yet my poor heart had
Its yearning aches, its unfulfilled desires.
    Love's balm is rest, but scorching are love's fires —
    The highest love is always strangely sad.

Why is it, Lord, that those who love Thee best
Because of love must share Thine agony?
Teresa's flaming heart cries out to Thee,
"From pain, my Loved One, never give me rest!"
    A sword of sorrow wounds Thy Mother's breast,
    And Thou, Love's King, art dead upon a tree.

He left His throne where burn the seraphim
To light on earth a fire that may not die;
Love made for Him a cross on which to lie,
And from a thorn-tree shaped a crown for Him.
    Long after in a cloister's chapel dim
    A nun knelt low and felt His Presence nigh.

She saw Him stand with bleeding heart aflame —
This burning and this bleeding heart I see:
It tells my heart what else were mystery,
This thorn-bound heart that in the vision came,
A symbol that shall evermore proclaim
That burning love must always bleeding be!

BUT TWO I LOVE*

James M. Hayes

But Two I love —
A King and Queen in Heaven above.
Had God made me
A man I now His priest would be,
And unto men
Appear as Christ on earth again.

But Two I love —
A King and Queen in Heaven above.
I am a nun,
The spouse of God's Eternal Son,
And men must see
The Mother of the King in me.

So may it be while all the ages run,
Christ in His priest and Mary in His nun.

* "My ambition is to be like the Blessed Virgin." This sentence is from a letter written by a Sister of Charity of Nazareth, and is the inspiration of this verse.

Editor's Note

MOTHER SAINT URBAN
Of the Bon 'Secours Sisters of Baltimore

James M. Hayes

'Twas in the dawn
She heard the summons for her soul's release.
She loved the dawn,
Its soft light, and its bird song and its peace.

Her day was done,
A day of labor that her love made sweet.
The Bridegroom called;
She waited for the coming of His Feet.

She is not gone;
She still will guide and help us with her prayer.
Because with God
She is with us — for God is everywhere.

OLD NUNS

James M. Hayes

Our Lady smiles on youthful nuns,
   She loves them well.
Our Lady smiles, and sunshine floods
   Each convent cell,
But fondest falls Our Lady's smile
   Where old nuns dwell.

Old nuns whose hearts are young with love
   For Mary's Son,
Old nuns whose prayers for faltering souls
   Have victory won,
Old nuns whose lives are beautiful
   With service done.

Their love a loveless world has saved
   From God's dread rod,
The paths where Sorrow walks with Sin
   Their feet have trod,
Their knees have worn the flags that pave
   The house of God.

Our Lady smiles on youthful nuns,
   She loves them well.
Our Lady smiles, and sunshine floods
   Each convent cell,
But fondest falls Our Lady's smile
   Where old nuns dwell.

SISTER MARY PHILOMENA*

James M. Hayes

A Tabor was her dying bed,
  With prayer and praise she passed away;
"It is not death," her sisters say,
  "She rests with God, she is not dead."

'Twas theirs to see her glorified,
  As saw of old the chosen three;
They did not think that death could be
  So beautiful until she died.

She walked the ways the lonely trod,
  She served the poor, she made her school
With faith and love the vestibule
  Whose portals opened unto God.

She could not make the canvas live,
  Nor could she strike the lyric string,
The songs of earth she could not sing,
  Nor to the marble beauty give.

A higher gift to her was given ——
  With Love's own hand to fashion souls,
To touch with beauty fadeless scrolls
  The Eyes of God shall read in Heaven.

* Sister Mary Philomena was a Sister of Mercy who organized and for many years directed Saint Gabriel's School in Chicago. Saint Gabriel's was the first free grade and high school for boys and girls in the United States.

Editor

MOTHER MARY XAVIER
On Her Golden Jubilee

BENJAMIN DIONYSIUS HILL, C.P.

'Twas a Jubilee day, our first Mother's first Daughter,
    When setting your face toward the Western afar,
You braved the long leagues of the storm-haunted water,
    To follow the shining of Mary, the Star.

On toiled the good ship, bringing nearer each morrow
    Its message of mercy, its burden of love:
Seven offerings of faith from the "Island of Sorrow"
    A mystical band with the seal of the dove.

But you were the chief of that virginal Seven,
    And lo, when their feet touched America's shore
'Twas the day your Saint Xavier had landed in heaven
    And the blessing he gave you abides evermore.

II

Again 'tis a jubilee day, dearest Mother!
    Your daughters stand up in this home of the free,
And bid to-day echo the joy of another
    Which dawned ere you followed the Star of the Sea.

'Twas the morn of your bridal. The troth you then plighted
    How faithfully kept, we your children attest.
You may count us by scores: we greet you united
    With happier scores who have gone to their rest.

[62]

This Jubilee Spousal — this calm Golden Wedding —
  Lights up like a sunset the grace-fruited past:
And we hail in the peace its sweet radiance is shedding
  A pledge of the glory that shall crown you at last.

Mother Mary Xavier Ward was the first novice professed by the foundress of the Sisters of Mercy, Mother Mary Catherine McAuley. Mother Xavier established the first convent of the Sisters of Mercy in the United States, at Pittsburgh in 1843.

Editor's Note

THE CONVENT GARDEN

Katherine Tynan Hinkson

The convent garden lies so near
   The road the people go,
If it was quiet you might hear
   The nuns talk merry and low.

Black London trees have made their screen
   From folk who pry and peer,
The sooty sparrows now begin
   Their talk of country cheer.

And round and round by two's and three's
   The nuns walk, praying still
For fighting men across the sea
   Who die to save them ill.

From the dear prison of her choice
   The young nun's thoughts are far;
She muses on the golden boys
   At all the fronts of war.

Now from her narrow Convent house
   She sees great ships go by,
And plucks the robe of God, her Spouse,
   To give them victory.

Under her robe her heart's abeat,
   Her maiden pulses stir,
At sound of marching in the street,
   To think they die for her.

And now beneath the veil and hood
 Her hidden eyes will glow,
The battle ardour's in her blood —
 If she might strike one blow.

And when she sleeps at last, perchance
 Her soul hath slipped away
To fields of Serbia and of France
 Until the dawn of day.

She wanders by the still moonbeam
 By dying and by dead.
And many a broken man will dream
 An angel lifts his head.

All day and night, as a sweet smoke,
 Her prayer ascends the skies,
That all her piteous fighting folk
 May walk in Paradise.

And still her innocent pulses stir,
 Her heart is proud and high,
To think that men should die for her —
 And the marching feet go by.

SISTER VERONICA

Margaret Holmes

Her life-path winds through shadowed ways,
   And many days
Are hidden deep in grief and pain
And drenched with sorrow's tears:
   And many nights, with saintly grace
Of heart and hand, she keeps her place
Where life and death stand face to face.

Whoe'er it needs, receives her care,
Together with her earnest prayer.
Unquestioning, serene and still,
She waits but for the Master's will.

And so whene'er the angel calls
   And twilight falls,
And this sweet soul within the boat
That sails the waveless sea
Is faring home; her kindly deeds
For other's woes, for other's needs,
Shall spring to life like buried seeds
Of lotus, and the darksome way
Be whiter than the whitest day;
And clouds of perfume shall arise
   To waft her into Paradise.

TO TWO LITTLE SISTERS OF THE POOR

ALINE KILMER

Sweet and humble and gladly poor,
The Grace of God came in at my door.

Sorrow and death were mine that day,
But the Grace of God came in to stay;

The Grace of God that spread its wings
Over all sad and pitiful things.

Sorrow turned to the touch of God,
Death became but His welcoming nod.

Grey-eyed, comforting, strong and brave,
You came to ask but instead you gave.

Quickly you came and went, you two,
But the Grace of God stayed after you.

BENEATH THE SANCTUARY LAMP

Elenita Thompson Kirkpatrick

Beneath the sanctuary lamp —
I saw her eyes
A-light with love divine and blue
As summer's evening skies.

Beneath the sanctuary lamp —
So young, so frail;
I saw her from the Bishop take
The convent's holy veil.

Beneath the sanctuary lamp —
Beside her bier
I passed the night in prayer and praise
Without a sob or tear.

Beneath the sanctuary lamp —
My daily tryst
I keep with her, and Heaven is near
For she is here with Christ.

THE CONVENT GARDEN

Marie Kirkwood

Rose bushes lean against the wall:
    They're weighty with their flowers.
They're beautiful throughout the day,
    They scent the night-time hours.

We're mignonettes, and candytufts,
    But no one half supposes
That they would pick us little folks
    When they could gather roses.

But when the month of June is gone
    And rose blooms fade and falter,
The nuns are glad for little plants
    To trim Our Lady's altar.

THE NUN

Shiel MacDara

O Einisheen O Dhua, your woman's voice is calling me
Across the width of the world to one remembered glen,
And all the imaged grace of you comes as of old, enthralling
me —
Oh, would I were beside you in our vale of dreams again!
To shepherd and to till for you, to harvest and to build for
you,
To diadem you queen upon a farmer's rugged throne:
So I have long been yearning, a thousand times have willed
for you —
But, ah, do dreams ever come true, my Einisheen, my own?

O Einisheen O Dhua, the wise and tender ways of you,
Your gentle voice of melody, your smile that I have blessed,
Have lit my every labor — sure, my heart has made its praise
of you
In trouble and in triumph like a song within my breast!
The calm and dear delight of you, the golden-crowned slim
height of you,
The step that kept such delicate time to Ruak the fiddler's
tune;
Oh, 'tis them again I'm seeing in my memory's raptured sight
of you
And my thoughts are all this minute one bright prayer for you
aroon. . . .

O Einisheen O Dhua, but what is this I hear of you?
What are the tidings chance has brought across the clearing
    sea?
Ah, privileged one, I might have known! Sure Mary's sign
    was clear on you —
Proudly I sing the holy truth: that 'tis a nun you'll be.
You have the veil and vows of Christ, you have espoused the
    Sacrificed —
His peace be always with you on the sainted way you go —
And pray a little prayer for me when kneeling in His House
    of Tryst,
That one day I may share afar the joy which you must know.

IN THE NUNS' GARDEN

Denis A. McCarthy

In the nuns' garden lean the lilies slender,
   In the nuns' garden crimson roses blow;
And many flowers, old fashioned, fair and tender,
   Along the paths in rich profusion grow.

But sweeter than the roses and the lilies
   That fill with beauty all the gay parterres,
The virgin flowers whose joyous duty still is
   To waft to God the perfume of their prayers!

In the nuns' garden, weary of his vagrance,
   Often the wanderer comes his woes to plead,
For in that place of purity and fragrance
   Are gentle hearts responsive to his need.

There mercy dwells among the crimson roses;
   There no one knocks upon the gate in vain;
For like the door of Heaven it never closes
   On human sorrow, or on human pain.

In the nuns' garden lean the lilies slender,
   And many a flower adorns the gay parterres,
But sweeter are the souls so pure and tender
   Who waft to God the perfume of their prayers!

SISTER MARGARET BOURGEOYS*

Thomas D'Arcy McGee

Dark is the light of Prophecy — no heavenly dews distill
On Sion's rock, on Jordan's vale, or Hermon's holy hill —
"Save us, O Lord!" the Psalmist cries, pouring his soul's
    complaint;
"Save us, O Lord! in these our days, for Israel has no Saint."
Not half so dark the sky of night, her starry hosts without,
As the night-time of the nations when God's living lamps go
    out.

But wondrous is the love of God, who sent His shining host,
From age to age, from race to race, from utmost coast to
    coast:
And wondrous 'twas in our own land — e'en on the spot we
    tread —
Ere yet the forest monarchs to the axe had bowed the head,
That in our very hour of dawn, a light for us was set,
Here on the royal mountain's side, whose lustre guides us yet.

'Tis pleasant in the gay green wood — so all the poets sing —
To breathe the very breath of flowers, and hear the sweet
    birds sing,
'Tis pleasant to shut out the world — behind their curtains
    green
To live and laugh, or muse and pray, forgotten and unseen;
But men or angels seldom saw a sight to heaven more dear,
Than Sister Margaret and her flock upon our hillside here.

* Sister Margaret Bourgeoys was the founder of the great Canadian
Order, "The Congregation of Our Lady." She organized her commun-
ity in the little village of Hochelaga, the site of the city of Montreal,
toward the middle of the Seventeenth Century.

Editor

From morn to eve a hum arose above the maple trees,
A hum of harmony and praise from Sister Margaret's bees;
Egyptian hue and speech uncouth grew fair and sweet when
    won
To sing the song of Mary, and to serve her Savior Son;
The courier halted on his path, the sentry on his round,
And bare-head blessed the holy nun who made it holy
    ground.

There came a day of tempest, where all was peace before —
The Huron war-cry rang dismay on Hochelaga's shore —
Then in that day all men confessed, with all man's humbled
    pride,
How brave a heart, till God's good time, a convent serge
    may hide.
The savage triumphed o'er the saint — a tiger in the fold —
But the mountain mission stands to-day! The Huron's tale
    is told!

Glory to God who sends His saints to all the ends of earth,
Wherever Adam's erring race have being or have birth,
Glory to God who sends His saints, our sunshine and our
    dew,
Through all the realms and nations of the Old World and the
    New,
Who perfumes the Pacific with His lily and His rose,
Who sent His holy ones to bless and bloom amid our snows!

SISTER AGATHA

Mary A. McMullen

Within a splendid home is missed a frank and joyous smile,
A fair young face undimmed by care, a heart untouched by
   guile,
And thoughtful, earnest eyes that seem to pierce the future
   far,
As through the night's blue depths looks down the clear eye
   of a star.

To that young heart sweet Mercy spoke from Heaven's
   portals high,
And in their weariness she heard earth's suffering children
   cry:
Then bidding friends and home adieu, she cast life's pleasures down,
To follow the anointed One Who wore the thorny crown.

Far from the loving hearts at home, her treasured household
   band,
In patient cheerfulness she toiled with brave, untiring hand;
And many straying souls looked up to her in hope and love,
And by her saintly life were led to think of God above.

The friendless suff'rer, tossing wild upon the couch of pain,
With aching limbs and throbbing heart and fever-heated
   brain,
Oft listened for her soothing voice, and grateful glances cast
Upon her sympathetic face and blessed her as she passed.

She fell beneath the fearful scourge whose pestilential breath
Sweeps o'er the sunny Southern land upon the wings of
    death;
Where friends from friends in terror fled, her fearless step
    had come,
And 'mid the dying and the dead the angels called her home.

Her hands are folded from their works of mercy and of love,
One saint the less is here below, one angel more above;
And many tears bedew the clay that folds in slumber calm
The fair young Sister far from home beneath the Southern
    palm.

IN THE LONGER NOVITIATE

CATHARINE McPARTLIN

Dear Lord of Life, if I will follow Thee,
Must I leave all that is most dear to me —
The love of humankind? If I must live
Deaf to their yearning call, what wilt Thou give
To still my human pang? Lord, let it be
Love's highest wish, their surer safety.

If I leave all, then the bright season's change
That with new stirring teaches me of strange
Inheritance of rapture — then the spring's
Sweet burgeoning and the soft whirr of wings
Shall be temptation. When with mighty lure
The Great Law summons, Lord, that I endure,
Feed with Thy Sacred Body from above
The white-flame hunger of the Greater Love.

If now I come, the silent aisles of peace
Shall bid youth's joy and woe forever cease;
No more the morning heights, the paths of air,
Up from the sudden caverns of despair.
Yet in the level roads shall be the Hill
Of Ecstasy, and at the Holy Will,
Down-droppings into dark. The long, dry years
Shall know the flowering of youth's hopes and fears.

I have come far. Yonder the cloistering trees
Send welcoming whispers on the ushering breeze.
The great world-forest signaled many ways —
I have lost time within its greenwood maze.

Listening I walk. Imperious, sweet the Voice,
Until there is no chance of doubt or choice.
Unto the waiting toil joyous I run —
Thy servant, Lord! Only Thy Will be done!

QUAINT RIDER
(*For a School Sister of Notre Dame*)

FRANCIS MAGUIRE

Though quaint indeed your riding habit—
Veil of midnight, frosty guimpe —
Still, madam, you outrun the rabbit,
Outshine the lamp.

For we, no longer to be fooled
By modest hands and downcast eyes,
Know that your way, the hardy schooled,
Traverses skies.

And even now, as here we meet you,
Demurest lady, wherever you are,
There on your ride to heaven we greet you —
Girl on a star!

LINES WRITTEN IN A NUNNERY CHAPEL

JAMES CLARENCE MANGAN

Me hither from moonlight
   A voice ever calls
Where pale pillars cluster
   And organ tones roll —
Nor sunlight nor moonlight
   E'er silvers these walls —
Lives here other lustre —
   The Light of the Soul.

Here budded and blossomed —
   Here faded and died —
Like brief blooming roses
   Earth's purest of pure!
Now ever embosomed
   In bliss they abide —
Oh! may, when life closes,
   My meed be as sure.

SISTER ANN RAPHAEL, S.N.D.

E. Mary

Her noblest poem was a life that bore
  On every page the seal of sanctity.
  The sweet-voiced singer may forgotten be;
The scientist who versed in Nature's lore,
Made it her dearest pleasure to explore
  Of seed and shell and star the mystery,
  And seemed to hold of Nature's heart the key,
May be remembered by us here no more.

But memory of the kindly, gracious word,
  The daily selfless giving of her best,
The life of prayerful calm beneath God's Eye —
  This is to Notre Dame her rich bequest,
By this to nobler impulse hearts are stirred,
  And leaving this she left what cannot die.

"SOEUR MONIQUE"
A Rondeau by Couperin

ALICE MEYNELL

Quiet form of silent nun,
What has given you to my inward eyes?
What has marked you, unknown one,
In the throngs of centuries
That mine ears do listen through?
This old master's melody
That expresses you;
This admired simplicity,
Tender, with a serious wit;
And two words, the name of it,
    "Soeur Monique."

And if sad the music is,
It is sad with mysteries
Of a small immortal thing
That the passing ages sing —
Simple music making mirth
Of the dying and the birth
Of the people of the earth.

No, not sad; we are beguiled,
Sad with living as we are;
Ours the sorrow, outpouring
Sad self on a selfless thing,
As our eyes and hearts are mild
With our sympathy for Spring,

With a pity sweet and wild
For the innocent and far,
With our sadness in a star,
Or our sadness in a child.

But two words and this sweet air.
    Soeur Monique,
Had he more who set you there?
Was his music-dream of you
Of some perfect nun he knew,
Or of some ideal, as true?

And I see you where you stand
With your life held in your hand
As a rosary of days.
And your thoughts in calm arrays,
And your innocent prayers are told
On your rosary of days.
And the young days and the old
With their quiet prayers did meet
When the chaplet was complete.

Did it vex you, the surmise
Of this wind of words, this storm of cries,
   Though you kept the silence so,
   In the storms of long ago,
   And you keep it, like a star?
   —Of the evils triumphing,
Strong, for all your perfect conquering,
   Silenced conqueror that you are?

[83]

And I wonder at your peace, I wonder.
Would it trouble you to know,
Tender soul, the world and sin
By your calm feet trodden under
    Long ago,
Living now, mighty to win?
And your feet are vanished like the snow.

Vanished; but the poet, he
In whose dream your face appears,
He who ranges unknown years
With your music in his heart,
Speaks to you familiarly
Where you keep apart,
And invents you as you were.
And your picture, O my nun!
Is a strangely easy one,
For the holy weed you wear,
For your hidden eyes and hidden hair,
And in picturing you I may
Scarcely go astray.

O the vague reality,
The mysterious certainty!
O strange truth of these my guesses
In the wide thought-wildernesses!
—Truth of one divined of many flowers;
Of one rainbow in the showers
Of the long-ago swift rain;
Of one tear of many tears
In some world-renownèd pain;

Of one daisy 'mid the centuries of sun;
Of a little living nun
In the garden of the years.

Yes, I am not far astray;
But I guess you as might one
Pausing when young March is grey,
In a violet-peopled day;
All his thoughts go out to places that he knew,
To his child home in the sun,
To the fields of his regret,
To one place i' the innocent March air,
By one olive, and invent
The familiar form and scent
Safely; a white violet
Certainly is there.

Soeur Monique, remember me.
'Tis not in the past alone
I am picturing you to be;
But my little friend, my own,
In my moment pray for me.
For another dream is mine,
And another dream is true,
    Sweeter even,
Of the little ones that shine
Lost within the light divine —
Of some meekest flower, or you,
In the fields of heaven.

MARCELA*

George Henry Miles

Was it wrong, dear Lady Abbess,
 That I spent the night in prayer,
That the rosary you gave me
 Numbered every bead a year?
I but wept until the watchman
 Pausing in the street below,
Slowly chimed the midnight ave,
 Then I gave to God my woe.

Thrice I sued the saints for slumber,
 Still I could not keep away
From the narrow window facing
 The lit chapel where he lay —
Where the funeral torches flickered
 Through the ever opening door,
As around their silent Poet,
 Passed the throng of rich and poor.

Yes, I went to sleep, dear Mother,
 But morning came so soon,
As I watched that lighted chapel
 Shining back upon the moon:
Once, methought, I lay beside him
 'Neath the sable and the gold,

* Sister Marcela de Carpio was the only daughter of Felix Lope de Vega, Spanish poet and dramatist. She was a nun of the Trinitarian Convent in Madrid, and was famous for her sanctity and poetry. John Hay — private secretary to Abraham Lincoln, and Secretary of State in the cabinets of Presidents McKinley and Theodore Roosevelt has translated one of her poems.

Editor

Bending o'er my minstrel father
    As I used in days of old.

And a light — the same that trembled
    O'er his lips and o'er his brow,
When he sang our San Isidora
    With the Angels at the plow —
And a smile — the same that shone there,
    When he bade the Mother mild
Hush the winds that shook the palm trees
    Rustling o'er her sleeping Child.

Oh, 'tis hard that all may follow
    The mute minstrel to his rest,
Save the nearest and the dearest,
    Save the daughter he loved best!
I alone, his own Marcela
    Can not touch dear Lope's bier,
Can not kiss the lips whose music
    None but Angels now may hear!

Still I feel, dear Lady Abbess,
    You will grant me what you may;
Since your smile first hailed me Novice
    It is fourteen years to-day:
Have I shrunk from fast or vigil,
    Have I failed at matin bell,
Have I clung to earthen image
    Since I bade the world farewell?

Nine long days I've heard the tolling
    Of the bells he loved to hear,

Nine long days I've heard the wailing
  Of Madrid around his bier;
And, to-day he will be buried
  For I catch the deepening hum
Of the people, and the stepping
  Of the soldiers as they come.

Never once I begged you lead me
  To the consecrated place,
Where between the triple tapers,
  I might gaze upon his face —
Grant me, then, sweet Lady Abbess
  Only this — but this, alas!
'Neath Marcela's cloister window
  Let her father's funeral pass.

Not one look, not one, I promise,
  For the princes in their might,
For the war-horse proudly curving
  To the spur of sworded knight:
Though all Spain in tears surround him
  I shall know her minstrel dead,
And my eyes — they will not wander
  Far from Lope's silver head.

Look, the chapel doors are parting,
  See the lifted torches shine,
And the horsemen and the footmen
  All the swarming pathways line.
Can it be! — these poor tears blind me —
  Ah, you know what I would pray,
And have granted ere I asked it —
  Yes, they come — they come this way.

TO A NUN DECORATED WITH THE IRON CROSS*

J. CORSON MILLER

The day was hot and the sun beat down
   Like a million tongues of fire;
The wounded lay in bloody heaps,
   Like broken bags of grain.
But one moved 'round like an angel bright,
   Through the blood and the stench and the mire,
With water for the parchéd throats,
   And prayers for the slain:
A woman, sworn to serve for Christ,
   She braved the leaden rain.

The guns belched forth a stream of flame,
   Till it seemed the jaws of hell
Oped wide upon the very earth
   To gulp God's creatures down.
Men dropped like grass from the mower's scythe,
   Died screaming as they fell,
And through the smoke the sunset turned
   From red to a ghastly brown.
A nun worked hard for Christ that day
   To win Love's golden crown.

* Sister Rosina of Kempton, a nurse at the western front since the
beginning of the First World War. In a battle near St. Mihiel she carried
seven wounded soldiers from the firing line. She also saved an officer
who was fast bleeding to death, and was herself struck by a bullet.

Author's Note

[89]

The winds of hate blew far and near,
    As when mad lions roar;
The vengeful gases ebbed and flowed,
    As Death held kingly sway.
A bullet struck nor halted her,
    She seemed to work the more,
Calling on Christ to lend His aid,
    And helping men to pray:
For Charity was in the look
    And garb she wore that day.

Jeanne d'Arc of France, immortal, sleeps,
    Greek Helen thrills the mind;
See! Dante's Beatrice laughs at Time,
    And Israel's Ruth knows fame.
Yet here's a woman men might sing
    Till Time's last link be twined,
Who soothed our poor humanity
    When War's fierce onslaught came.
Methinks the gentle Christ Himself
    Must love and bless her name.

SAINT BRIGID
(*The First Irish Nun*)

Rosa Mulholland (Lady Gilbert)

'Mid dewy pastures girdled with blue air,
 Where ruddy kine the limpid water drink,
Through violet-purpled woods of green Kildare,
 'Neath rainbow skies, by tinkling rivulet's brink,
O Brigid, young, thy tender snow-white feet
 In days of old on breezy morns and eves
Wandered through labyrinths of sun and shade,
   Thy face so innocent-sweet
 Shining with love that neither joys nor grieves
Save as the angels, meek and holy maid!

With white fire in thy hand that burned no man,
 But cleansed and warmed where'er its ray might fall,
Nor ever wasted low, or needed fan,
 Thou walk'st at eve among the oak-trees tall.
There thou didst chant thy vespers, while each star
 Grew brighter listening through the leafy screen.
Then ceased the song-bird all his love-notes soft,
   His music near or far,
 Hushing his passion 'mid the sombre green
To let thy peaceful whispers float aloft.

And still from heavenly choirs thou steal'st by night
 To tell sweet *Aves* in the woods unseen,
To tend the shrine-lamps with thy *flambeau* white
 And set thy tender footprints on the green.
Thus sing our birds with holy note and pure,

As though the love of angels were their theme;
Thus burn to throbbing flame our sacred fires
With heats that still endure;
Thence hath our daffodil its golden gleam,
From thy dear mindfulness that never tires!

EPITHALAMIUM
(*For the Clothing of a Nun*)

HELENE MULLINS

No, she does not falter
　On her wedding day.
Lead her to the altar,
　In her bride's array.

Give away her gems;
　Him she goes to wed
Has but thorny stems
　Wreathed upon His head.

Give away her money
　And her golden boots,
She must thrive on honey
　And bitter berry-roots.

Give her books away,
　All her things of beauty;
She shall pass each day
　In some humble duty.

'Tis the hour, musicians!
　Strike the joyous chords.
On her finger glistens
　A brave ring of the Lord's.

Beautiful and doomed,
　She takes the Bridegroom's kisses.

The chapel is perfumed
  With lily and narcissus.

Though lacking gems and laces,
  In ecstasy she lives;
But see the mournful faces
  Of her relatives.

See the tears they keep
  Passionately shedding.
Why do people weep
  At a young girl's wedding?

SISTER MARY CONCEPTIA

Helene Mullins

O lady with the luminous sombre eyes,
  Your quaint medieval costume suits you well;
Yet I have never thought it very wise
  That life be sacrificed to make a shell
For the most entrancing art. Oh, realize
  Your fate is a sadder thing than words can tell!
Why do you rise to the sound of a bell in the cold
  Dim light of the dawn, and fill the Winter day
With futile tasks no one will pause to behold?
  I dream you are not so well content as you say,
That you'll some day clothe yourself in silver and gold,
And turn from your cell to a prince who will steal you away.

You have guessed my secret and I bid you keep
  It even as I have done; and I bid you hear
What you have not guessed. My Lord has seen me weep,
  And has leaned from Heaven to tell me He is near;
I have felt His hands upon me in my sleep,
  I have laid my murmuring mouth against His ear.
I am scarcely aware of the daily tasks I do,
  My eyes are set upon a seat of ivory
And a crown of gold and a robe of summer blue,
  And the Lord of my heart will keep these things for me,
Till my blundering youth is faithfully gone through,
And my wisdom formed out of pain and poverty.

A FIRE SHALL BURN BEFORE HIM *

BENJAMIN FRANCIS MUSSER

The living sacrifice, the pyre
That lighted heav'n that night,
An outwardly consuming fire
Was to the inward light
That lit their hearts disparity;
So burns the heart of Charity.

Elijah in his flaming car
Was swift to heaven drawn;
But they, each one a glowing star,
Still shine across the dawn
To light the way ere we expire,
Poor moths entranced by earthy fire.

The Pentecostal tongues of flame
From God to men were given;
But they, when that their message came,
Gave tongues of flame to heaven.
May we with little orphans see
The love that burns in Charity

* In memory of six Sisters of Charity of the Incarnate Word, burned to
death while rescuing over a hundred orphans, October 30, 1912.

Author

ELDERLY NUN

Benjamin Francis Musser

Not hers the young nun's quest to ride
  On heaven-flung ecstasies,
To fret her being with mortified
  And quaint austerities.

First fervor still remains, but now
  It broods in quiet gaze
Focused on Him; she keeps her vow
  In untormented ways.

Her hands lie folded that have toiled
  In service of the King;
Still is her wedding robe unsoiled,
  And chaste her marriage ring.

Little she speaks — her conversation
  Is all in heaven with Him
In wordless words' reverberation
  Beyond the interim.

Serene she waits in placid cell,
  Lamp trimmed, all things in order,
For call more sweet than chapel bell
  Ringing at Heaven's border.

A FRAGMENT FROM SAINT GREGORY NAZIANZEN*

John Henry Newman

As, when the hand some mimic form would paint,
It marks its purpose first in shadows faint,
And next, its store of varied hues applies,
Till outlines fade, and the full limbs arise;
So in the earlier school of sacred lore
The Virgin-life no claim of honor bore,
While in Religion's youth the Law held sway,
And traced in symbols dim that better way.
But, when the Christ came by a Virgin-birth —
His radiant passage from high Heaven to earth —
And, spurning father for His mortal state,
Did Eve and all her daughters consecrate,
Solved fleshly laws, and in the letter's place
Gave us the Spirit and the Word of Grace,
Then shone the glorious Celibate at length,
Robed in the dazzling lightnings of its strength,
Surpassing spells of earth and marriage vow,
As soul the body, heaven this world below,
The eternal peace of saints life's troubled span,
And the high Throne of God, the haunts of man.
So now there circles round the King of Light
A heaven on earth, a blameless court and bright,
Aiming as emblems of their God to shine,
Christ in their heart, and on their brow His Sign, —
Soft funeral lights in the world's twilight dim,
Loving their God and ever loved by Him.

* This extract applies not only to nuns, but to all who take the vow of
virginity for the sake of God.

Editor's Note

RESIGNATION

Julia Claire O'Connor

Goodby was not an easy word to voice.
And when you left I could not hide my tears,
Made poignant by the thought of empty years
Alone. My hopes rebelled against your choice.
But your young heart knew purer love than mine.
Your lips were meant to move in cloistered prayer.
I did not bid you stay; I would not dare
Compete against a Love which is divine.

Now when I see you kneel before His Cross
To consecrate yourself — your every breath
With vows which covet no release but death,
A sudden calm supplants my sense of loss.
For in your sacrifice I claim a part:
I lay beside your life, my lonely heart.

A SISTER

A. Page, C.S.C.

I am the bride of Christ, she said
    By candle light I have been wed
        Unto the King of Kings.
The angels were my retinue;
    My bridal dress of white and blue,
        And so my heart just sings.

Upon the Sacred Heart's own day
    My brother own gave me away
        Unto his Brother-Love.
My bridal veil, the shroud of night,
    But Love had lit a vigil light
        In my soul by His Dove.

So now my lips must sing His praise,
    My tongue proclaim His gracious ways,
        My eyes seek only Christ,
My mind be fixed on Him alone
    My heart rest only at His throne,
        By His Love all sufficed!

Perfect me, Virgin Lover pure,
    And let me pass with steps more sure
        Along the narrow way:
And ever Thou abide with me,
    And let Thy heart my cloister be
        Till shadows pass away.

SISTER AND NUN

A. Page, C.S.C.

A nun is a city builded
About a citadel,
A walléd silent city,
Where God alone may dwell;
A sister, a little village
Christ sets beside the way,
Where pilgrims may find shelter
And learn to love and pray.

A nun is a vigil lighted
Before the Master's throne,
And that it may burn brightly,
It needs must burn alone;
A sister, a candle gleaming
In Earth's dull window pane,
That men may be reminded
Of Christ and His sweet reign.

A nun is a chalice lifted
To slake a thirst divine:
A sister, a host fragmented
To feed the twigs of His vine:
The nun, a sister who toileth
At the quiet loom of prayer;
The sister, a nun whose cloister
Is other people's care.

And one from her shadowed chapel,
And one from classroom or ward,
Shall each be called by the Master,
Shall each receive His applaud:
And sister and nun together
Shall rest at the feet of God,
Though one sought Him in the mountains
And one found Him in the clod.

HAIL VIRGIN IN VIRGINITY A SPOUSE
From *Deliciae Sapientiae*

COVENTRY PATMORE

Love, light for me
Thy ruddiest blazing torch,
That I, albeit a beggar by the Porch
Of the glad Palace of Virginity,
May gaze within and sing the pomp I see;
For, crowned with roses all,
'Tis there, O Love, they keep thy festival!

* * * * * * * * * *

O, hear
From the harps they bore from Earth, five-strung, what
    music springs,
While the glad Spirits chide
The wondering strings!
And how the shining sacrificial Choirs,
Offering for aye their dearest hearts' desires,
Which to their hearts come back beatified,
Hymn, the bright aisles along,
The nuptial song,
Song ever new to us and them, that saith,
"Hail Virgin in Virginity a Spouse!"
Heard first below
Within the little house
At Nazareth;

Heard yet in many a cell where brides of Christ
Lie hid, emparadised,
And where, although
By the hour 'tis night,
There's light,
The Day still lingering in the lap of snow.

UNHEEDED VOCATION

Eleanore L. Perry

You should have walked those cooler garden ways
With others, whose low, sweet-toned voices drift
Across the silken stillness of the days,
And farther down, where twilight's shadows shift.
You should have known the high, swift, rushing sweep
Of singing wings that pass by in the night,
And felt the palest amber call of deep
Far-gleaming prayers, from blue stars burning white. . . .

You have not loved enough the garden ways,
And you have followed other voices now.
So, gaily, shall you dance on down the days
And never know the dear pain of their vow;
Your golden hair shall always glint the sun,
But lovelier far you would have been — a nun.

THE NUN'S LOT
From *Héloise and Abélard*

ALEXANDER POPE

How happy is the blameless vestal's lot!
The world forgotten, by the world forgot;
Eternal sunshine of the spotless mind,
Each prayer accepted, and each wish resigned;
Labour and rest, that equal periods keep;
Obedient slumbers that can wake and weep;
Desires composed, affections ever even;
Tears that delight, and sighs that waft to heaven.
Grace shines around her with serenest beams,
And whispering angels prompt her golden dreams.
For her the unfading rose of Eden blooms,
And wings of seraphs shed divine perfumes;
For her the Spouse prepares the bridal ring:
For her white virgins hymeneals sing;
To sounds of heavenly harps she dies away,
And melts in visions of eternal day.

DEATH IN CARMEL
For Mother Paula of the Mother of God

Jessica Powers

I was in a garden, she said,
On Mary's mountain,
And a Child was there,
And we played by a white fountain.

I sang to Him out of my heart
(For a Child loves singing)
And His Mother smiled at the two
To her mantle clinging.

I found Him little gifts
As we played together:
Flowers and colored stones
And a fallen feather.

We learned the words of life
From the primer of sorrow:
Parting and pain, and the death
Of a dark tomorrow.

The Child taught me the words
And the synonyms thereof,
And the meaning of every word
Was love.

I was in one garden, she said,
And now I am in another,

And a Child is here
Asleep near His young Mother.

I have a three-fold gift
My love can bring Him,
And each gift is a vow
And a song to sing Him.

I know this place, she said,
I am not a stranger.
And she knelt by the three Kings
At a shining manger.

DEATH OF SAINT THERESE OF LISIEUX
(A Carmelite Nun)

Jessica Powers

Winter, her life was past. To her charmed sill
The turtle-dove, prophetic, came to coo,
And through the odorous gardens of Lisieux
Close on the syllables of death's "Be still"
There came the love song of the Canticles:
"Arise, make haste, my love, my beautiful one
And come." In meadows amorous with the sun
Love met her to the welcome of the bells.

Thérèse, how true it is past all forgetting
That nothing matters save a precious death.
It is the jewel of which life is the setting,
Life is the clay, and it the shining breath.
And he like thee who makes his life its slave
Finds roses for all mankind in his grave.

A LEGEND OF PROVENCE *
(*Selections*)

ADELAIDE ANNE PROCTOR

Of all the nuns no heart was half so light,
No eyelids veiling glances half so bright,
No step that glided with such noiseless feet,
No face that looked so tender and so sweet,
No voice that rose in choir so pure, so clear,
No heart to all the others half so dear,
So surely touched by others' pain or woe,
(Guessing the grief her young life could not know)
No soul in childlike faith so undefiled,
As Sister Angela's, the "Convent Child."
For thus they loved to call her. She had known
No home, no love, no kindred, save their own.
An orphan to their tender nursing given,
Child, plaything, pupil, now the Bride of Heaven.

*   *   *

One night came straggling soldiers, with their load
Of wounded, dying comrades; and the band,
Half pleading, yet as if they could command,
Summoned the trembling Sisters, craved their care,
Then rode away and left the wounded there.
But soon compassion bade all fear depart,
And bidding every Sister do her part
Some prepare simples, healing salves or bands,
The Abbess chose the more experienced hands
To dress the wounds needing most skilful care;
Yet even the youngest novice took her share.

* This legend is found in the "Glories of Mary" by Saint Alphonsus
Liguori. Before Saint Alphonsus it was told by Cesarius and Father Rhio.
Editor

To Angela who had but ready will
And tender pity, yet no special skill,
Was given the charge of a young foreign knight,
Whose wounds were painful, but whose danger slight.
Day after day she watched beside his bed,
And first in hushed repose the hours fled:
His feverish moans alone the silence stirred,
Or her soft voice, uttering some pious word.
At last the fever left him; day by day
The hours, no longer silent, passed away.
What could she speak of? First to still his plaints,
She told him legends of the martyred saints;
Describing the pangs, which through God's plenteous
    grace,
Had gained their souls so high and bright a place.
This pious artifice soon found success —
Or so she fancied — for he murmured less.

      ✧   ✧   ✧

The knight unwearied listened; till at last,
He too described the glories of his past;
Tourney and joust, and pageant bright and fair,
And all the lovely ladies who were there.
But half incredulous she heard. Could this —
This be this world? this place of love and bliss!
Where then was hid the strange and hideous charm,
That never failed to bring the gazer harm?
She crossed herself, yet asked and listened still,
And still the knight described with all his skill
The glorious world of joy, all joys above,
Transfigured in the golden mist of love.

    ✧   ✧   ✧

So days went on until the convent gate
Opened one night. Who durst go forth so late?
Across the moonlit grass, with stealthy tread,
Two silent, shrouded figures passed and fled.
And all was silent, save the moaning seas,
That sobbed and pleaded, and a wailing breeze
That sighed among the perfumed hawthorn trees.

❈ ❈ ❈

Years fled . . .
At last a yearning seemed to fill her soul,
A longing that was stronger than control:
Once more, just once again to see the place
That knew her young and innocent; to retrace
The long and weary southern path; to gaze
Upon the haven of her childish days;
Once more beneath the convent roof to lie;
Once more to look upon her home — and die.

❈ ❈ ❈

Crouching against the iron gate, she laid
Her weary head against the bars, and prayed;
But nearer footsteps drew, then seemed to wait;
And then she heard the opening of the gate,
And saw the withered face, on which awoke
Pity and sorrow, as the portress spoke,
And asked the stranger's bidding: "Take me in,"
She faltered, "Sister Monica, from sin,
And sorrow and despair, that will not cease;
Oh, take me in, and let me die in peace!"
With soothing words the sister bade her wait,

Until she brought the key to unbar the gate.
The beggar tried to thank her as she lay,
And heard the echoing footsteps die away.
But what soft voice was that which sounded near,
And stirred strange trouble in her heart to hear?
She raised her head; she saw — she seemed to know
A face that came from long, long years ago;
Herself; yet not as when she fled away,
The young and blooming novice, fair and gay,
But a grave woman, gentle and serene:
The outcast knew it — *what she might have been.*
But as she gazed and gazed, a radiance bright
Filled all the place with strange and sudden light;
The nun was there no longer, but instead,
A figure with a circle round her head,
A ring of glory; and a face so meek,
So soft, so tender ———— Angela strove to speak,
And stretched her hands out, crying, "Mary mild,
Mother of Mercy, help, help me! — help your child!"
And Mary answered, "From thy bitter past,
Welcome, my child! oh, welcome home at last!
I filled thy place. Thy flight is known to none,
For all thy daily duties I have done;
Gathered thy flowers, and prayed and sung and slept;
Didst thou not know, poor child, *thy place was kept*?
Kind hearts are here; yet would the tenderest one
Have limits to its mercy; God has none.
And man's forgiveness may be true and sweet,
But yet he stoops to give it. More complete
Is Love that lays forgiveness at thy feet,
And pleads with thee to raise it. Only Heaven
Means *crowned,* not *vanquished,* when it says 'Forgiven!'"
Back hurried Sister Monica; but where

Was the poor beggar she left lying there?
Gone; and she searched in vain, and sought the place
For that wan woman, with the piteous face:
But only Angela at the gateway stood,
Laden with hawthorn blossoms from the wood.
And never did a day pass by again,
But the old portress, with a sigh of pain,
Would sorrow for her loitering: with a prayer
That the poor beggar, in her wild despair
Might not have come to any ill; and when
She ended, "God forgive her." Then
Did Angela bow her head and say "Amen!"

S. M. S.*
(*Sister Mary Stanislaus, O.P.*)

PATRICK AUGUSTINE SHEEHAN

I never knew thee child; But this I knew:
Thou camest from starred spaces to this world
With all thy spirit's faculties unfurled,
And thy great sponsor, music, promptly drew
From his large repertory, faultless, true,
A welcome from thy father, poet herald
Of May and pink May-blossoms lightly curled
To hold the chaliced sweetness of the dew.

And thou, the heiress of his wealth of song,
Poured all thy gold in streams of liquid light —
Doubly refined by all thy faith and love.
Lest thou shouldst cheat the vast expectant throng
Of one fine slender note, one music mite,
Singing thou soarest to the choirs above.

---

* Sister Mary Stanislaus was the daughter of the poet, Denis Florence MacCarthy the translator of Calderon and the author of the popular and lovely lyric "Waiting for the May." Her voice in song was of exceptional sweetness.

Editor

A SONG OF NUNS

James Shirley

O fly, my soul! What hangs upon
 Thy drooping wings,
And weighs them down
With love of gaudy mortal things?

The sun is now the East! each shade
 As he doth rise
Is shorter made
 That earth may lessen to our eyes.

Oh, be but careless then, and play
 Until the Star of Peace
Hide all his beams in dark recess,
Poor pilgrims needs must lose their way
When all the shadows do increase.

THE FIRST SNOWFALL
The Bees of Saint Rita, an Augustinian Nun

CHARLES WARREN STODDARD

Blue dome above us, marvellous hive
Opaline, crystalline, all alive
With the white bees of Blessed Rita!

If but these feathery flakes might store
Honey of Hybla in lucent comb,
Bee-like; if only the azure dome
Might harbor and house them more and more,
So that the seeker easily sees
Ever the delicate airy things
Fluttering with invisible wings —
Feathery flakes like bevies of bees —
Would they better us then, I wonder?
Would they even cover us under
Canopies of immaculate white?
Lodge us in little cells asunder —
Separate cells of honeyed delight.

Could they but sweeten the lips of song,
Chilling a passion, righting a wrong;
Purging a blemish, blotting a stain:
Making the tarnished heart clean again —
Then might we pluck away the leaven
Leavening all that else were beautiful:
Then might the wayward ones grow dutiful:

Looking above him to discover,
Flake upon flake, the clouds that hover,
Filling the happy hive of heaven
With the white bees of Blessed Rita!*

* The exquisite legend of Saint Rita which suggests this poem relates that all her life a swarm of white bees bore her company. They went with her to the Augustinian convent. After six centuries the wonder of Saint Rita's bees continues. In the convent of Cascia, hidden in the ancient wall between the cell of the Saint and the room where her body rests incorrupt, the descendants of the first bees live until this day. They are always fifteen in number; they are a trifle larger than the ordinary bee; their hum is different; they do not sting; and the species to which they belong has never been determined. They come out of their hives on Good Friday and return in May, after the Saint's feast, when they close their cells with a veil of white wax.

Editor

TO MY NUN SISTER

E. P. TIVNAN, S.J.

Methought I saw a wondrous throng,
And on mine ears a wondrous song
Fell strangely sweet and soothingly.
And lo, each spirit passing me
From earth to Heaven, with jealous care
Bore, every one, a star more fair
And sparkling with a clearer light
Than ever star on wintry night,
Straight to the great King's mighty Seat,
With hymn of adoration meet.
And when at length I trembling dared
Ask one why thus each spirit fared,
And what each precious load might be,
He said, "Thy sister's prayers for thee."
The vision straightway vanishéd,
And then there rose up in its stead
A sanctuary far away
Where other angels, kneeling, pray.
And there I saw thee in the dawn,
And knew whence came the strength newborn,
To rise and battle through the day,
For that thy prayers are mine alway.

II

TRIBUTES FROM POETS
WHO ARE NOT CATHOLIC*

* There are many translations of poems about nuns by distinguished English and American poets who are not Catholics. Among these are Lord Byron, Longfellow, John Hay, Felicia D. Hemans. As translations do not come within the scope of this work, they are not included. Far greater than that of his translation is the tribute Lord Byron paid to nuns when he sent his daughter to them for her education. "I am educating my natural daughter a strict Catholic in a convent of Romagna.... I incline myself very much to the Catholic doctrine." Life, Letters, and Journals of Lord Byron, by Thomas Moore. p. 551.

YOUNG NUN

GRACE NOLL CROWELL

She is so young for this grave sacrifice!
I wonder by what winding roads she came
To these dark corridors? Some pay the price,
And 'tis not strange; but what white blowing flame
Drove her before it? What importunate voice
Pierced youth's wild delirium and drew
Her forward to this passionate high choice
Of service to a church a lifetime through?

The soft curves of her body hide beneath
The folds of her dark habit; yet her slim
Bright youthfulness is like a silver sheath.
Was there some lover? Does she think of him?
Or is that luminous fire in her eyes,
That still white light upon her lifted face,
A love, beyond earth's passions and surprise,
Set like a candle flame to light this place?

SAINT ITE*
(An Irish Nun)

ROBIN FLOWER

He came to me
A little before morning, through the night
And lay between my breasts until day light.

How helplessly
Lay the small limbs, the fallen head of gold,
The little hands that clasped and could not hold.

I spoke no word,
Lest sleep's light-feathered wing should lift and fly
From this low earth to that steep heavenly sky.

And when He stirred
And opened frightened eyes and called for rest,
I set Him wailing to my maiden breast.

And thence He drew,
With soft stirred lips and clutching hands that strove,
Sweet mortal milk of more than mortal love.

When morning grew
Far in the East and the world woke from rest,
The King of Stars was quiet on my breast.

* Said Ite, "I will take nothing from my Lord save He give me His Son
in fashion of a babe that I may nurse Him." Then came the angel that
was wont to do service about her. " 'Tis good time," said she to him.
Then said the angel to her, "That thou askest shall be granted thee,"
and Christ came to her in fashion of a babe.—*The Comment of the
Feilire of Oingus.*

SOEUR FIDELE

Frances Gill

Sister Fidèle stands at the convent gate —
Her cool old hands like frailest lace.
Lace-like too, the woven wrinkled lines
That quaintly pattern her old face.
She smiled her welcome to our dropping coins.
"You wish to see the garden, I suppose.
This way, please ladies." Her old knees
Make every genuflection as she goes
Beneath the arch where swings the Crucifix.
"The lime trees are the oldest; they are grown
In France, and carried here in boats.
How long ago? That Madame, is not known.
These are our fuchsias brought to us from Spain.
The holy Abbess always tended them,
But I do now." She stopped to hide a tear,
And pick a leaf from her dark garment's hem.
"This our rose. We call it Maria's,
It blooms so well. It is so very red —
As if it were the very precious blood,"
She crossed herself here, "that Jesus shed.
The wall is old? Oh, yes, a thousand years
Have passed since it was builded here.
Our sainted Mother led the nuns
To set a feast for Charlemagne each year.
Our history? Ah, Madame, time to us
Is not of years and months. Our yesterdays
Are centuries ago. The convent's range
Is from Saint Peter to Eternity:
'Tis only we poor nuns who change —

No, do not thank me — It's my work to show
The garden to the guests who come and go.
I'll leave you at the chapel, where you may
If you should care to, pause, to rest and pray."

Her wiry wrinkled hand, her sweet old face,
Her dignity, her patience, her quiet and holy **grace,**
Were all the spirit of the holy place.
The thought of her, eight thousand miles away,
Strengthens me in her faith, here each day.

TO A NUN

MARY TERRY GILL

I may not hold to sacred strain
That made you different from your kind,
That fostered in your youthful brain
One deep-grooved sacrificial line
That barred the door of earthly things; that overcame
The human urge — Love and Life's renewing power
To live in other lives again —
A loss you count as sacred dower.

And yet your passion is to me
A "white fire" gleam of life divine;
A beacon set that I may see
And long to serve in part this task of thine —
This task for child and church; for poor and wretched blind,
And with it all to be serene — so gentle and so kind.

TO THE URSULINES*

Caroline Gilman

Oh, pure and gentle ones, within your ark
　　　Securely rest!
Blue be the sky above — your quiet bark
　　　By soft winds blest!

Still toil in duty, and commune with Heaven,
　　　World-weaned and free;
God to His humblest creatures room has given
　　　And space to be:
Space for the eagle in the vaulted sky
　　　To plume his wing —
Space for the ring-dove by her young to lie
　　　And softly sing —
Space for the sunflower, bright with yellow glow
　　　To court the sky —
Space for the violet, where the wild woods grow
　　　To live and die.
Space for the ocean in its giant might,
　　　To swell and rave —

* In the middle years of the nineteenth century a society was formed
for the purpose of crushing the Catholic Church in the United States.
It is known in history as the Know Nothing Society. Its ignorant and
misguided members burnt the Ursuline Convent in Charlestown, Massa-
chusetts, and did much damage to Catholic institutions in the East. The
writer of this poem was a Boston lady, the wife of the Reverend Samuel
Gilman, a noted preacher and writer of the Unitarian Church. She knew
the Ursulines, and her poem expresses the appreciation and regard of
the educated and respectable Protestants of the day for our Catholic
Sisters. Mrs. Gilman left Boston to make her home in Charleston, South
Carolina. Her life and letters and poems were published in 1941 in a
book, *A Balcony in Charleston.*

Editor

Space for the sun to tread his path in might
          And golden pride —
Space for the glow-worm, calling by her light,
          Love to her side.
Then, pure and gentle ones, within your ark
          Securely rest!
Blue be the skies above, and your still bark
          By kind winds blest.

SISTER SAINT LUKE

John Hay

She lived shut in by flowers and trees
And shade of gentle bigotries.
On this side lay the tractless sea,
On that the great world's mystery;
But all unseen and all unguessed
They could not break upon her rest.
The world's far splendors gleamed and flashed,
Afar the wild seas foamed and dashed:
But in her small dull Paradise,
Safe housed from rapture or surprise,
Nor day nor night had power to fright
The peace of God that filled her eyes.

THE BLIND NUN*

Thomas S. Jones, Jr.

A nun green-girdled in a forest tower
Gave praise that prayer had made her blind eyes new,
   And to her fern-wreathed lattice swiftly drew
   When thrushes call the dawn's cool silver hour:
   She saw beyond pale apple-boughs in flower
A dying moon and pastures pearled with dew,
Then where the hill-tops turned to lilac blue,
The red sun rising, fierce with golden power.

Yet lest the glowing world become too dear,
   White Dara prayed that darkness veil her sight,
   And closed the casement with an ivory rod:
Like shadows faded mountain, wood, and mere,
   But fairer than the sun or moon's strange light,
   Across her blindness shone the Face of God.

* Sister Dara was a nun in the convent of Saint Brigid of Kildare.

Editor

SAINT TERESA
(*A Carmelite Nun*)

Thomas S. Jones, Jr.

"Basil, rosemary, rue and lavender!
　　The well is dry, the water-wheels are still,
　　The river can no longer sluice the mill:
How shall the flowers in my heart's garden stir?"*
"When self shall sleep within a sepulchre,
　　Rain from the sky and healing dew shall fill
　　Each withered path, and there may walk at will
Love seen by Mary as a gardener.

"Along the border violets will spread,
　　Humility and lilies light the grass,
　　　Though snow fall early and the spring be late;
But where the bower of roses blossoms red
　　With thy heart's blood, there shall the Lover pass
　　　And there the Keeper of the Stars will wait."

* For twelve years Saint Teresa was in a state of spiritual dryness. It was a period of suffering and warfare and, at times, of inexpressible bitterness. Celestial joys deserted her, consolations disappeared, her sweetness in prayer was changed to aridity. She did not lose hope, but prayed and waited and abandoned herself into the hands of God. This is a consolation to the much-tried soul who treads a similar path.

Editor

THE NUN OF NIDAROS

HENRY WADSWORTH LONGFELLOW

In the convent of Dronthein,
Alone in her chamber
Knelt Astrid the Abbess,
At Midnight adoring,
Beseeching, entreating
The Virgin and Mother.

She heard in the silence
The voice of one speaking,
Without in the darkness.
In gusts of the night wind
Now louder, now nearer,
Now lost in the distance.

The voice of a stranger
It seemed as she listened,
Of some one who answered,
Beseeching, imploring,
A cry from afar off
She could not distinguish.

The voice of Saint John,*
The beloved disciple,
Who wandered and waited
The Master's appearance,
Alone in the darkness,
Unsheltered and friendless.

* Because of Our Lord's words (John, XXI, 23) it was believed by many
that Saint John is to remain in the world until the second coming of
Christ. This tradition has no ground in Catholic belief.

Editor

"It is accepted
The angry defiance,
The challenge of battle!
It is accepted,
But not with the weapons
Of war that thou wieldest!

"Cross against corslet,
Love against hatred,
Peace-cry for war cry!
Patience is powerful:
He that overcometh
Hath power o'er the nations.

"As torrents in summer,
Half dried in their channels,
Suddenly rise, though the
Sky is still cloudless,
For rain has been falling,
Far off at their fountains.

"So hearts that are fainting
Grow full to o'erflowing,
And they that behold it
Marvel and know not
That God at their fountains
Far off has been raining!

"Stronger than steel
Is the sword of the Spirit;
Swifter than arrows
The light of the truth is,

Greater than anger
Is love, and subdueth!

"Thou art a phantom
A shape of the mist,
A shape of the brumal
Rain, and the darkness
Fearful and formless;
Day dawns and thou art not!

"The dawn is not distant,
Nor is the night starless;
Love is eternal!
God is still God, and
His faith shall not fail us;
Christ is eternal!"

A LITTLE NUN

Edith Loomis

A little nun in habit white,
Gazed at the noon-bright skies.
"The only blue that I may wear,
Is in my eyes."

A little nun in habit grey
Stooped to a flower's grace.
"The only beauty I may show,
Is in my face."

A little nun in habit black,
Yearned toward the sunset's red.
Said she: "I'll have a flame-pink cloud
When I am dead."

SAINT BRIDE'S LULLABY*

Fiona Macleod (William Sharp)

Oh, Baby Christ, so dear to me,
    Sang Briget Bride:
How sweet thou art,
My baby dear,
Heart of My heart!

Heavy her body was with thee,
Mary, beloved of One in Three —
    Sang Briget Bride —
Mary, who bore thee, little lad:
But light her heart was, light and glad
With God's love clad.

Sit on my knee,
    Sang Briget Bride:
Sit here
O Baby dear,
Close to my heart, my heart:
For I thy foster mother am,
My helpless lamb!
O have no fear,
    Sang good Saint Bride.

* In Gaelic legend St. Bride who is called "Mary of the Gael" is said
to have been present at the Divine Birth. In the Gaelic language there is
no such name as Brigid. The name is Bree-id, Breege and more com-
monly Bride.

Editor

None, none,
No fear have I:
So let me cling
Close to thy side
While thou dost sing
O Briget Bride!
My Lord, my Prince, I sing:
My Baby dear, my King!
  Sang Briget Bride.

A SISTER OF CHARITY COMFORTS
A WOUNDED SOLDIER
From Lucile

OWEN MEREDITH (ROBERT, LORD LYTTON)

               "A nun has no nation.
Wherever man suffers or woman may soothe,
There her land! there her kindred!
            O, was it spoken,
'Go ye forth, heal the sick, lift the low, bind the broken!'
Of the body alone? Is our mission then done,
When we leave the bruised hearts, if we bind the bruised
    bone?
Nay, is not the mission of mercy twofold?
Whence twofold, perchance, are the powers which we hold
To fulfil it, of Heaven! For Heaven doth still
To us, Sisters, it may be who seek it, send skill
Won with long intercourse with affliction, the art
Helped of Heaven, to bind up the broken of heart."

THE MISSION OF SISTER SERAPHINE,
A SISTER OF CHARITY
From Lucile

OWEN MEREDITH (ROBERT, LORD LYTTON)

                    Her mission accomplished is o'er.
The mission of genius on earth! To uplift,
Purify and confirm by its own gracious gift,
The world, in despite of the world's dull endeavor
To degrade and drag down, and oppose it for ever.
The mission of genius: To watch, and to wait,
To renew, to redeem, and to regenerate.
The mission of woman on earth! permitted to bruise
The head of the serpent, and sweetly infuse
Through the sorrow and sin of earth's registered curse,
The blessing which mitigates all: born to nurse
And to soothe, and to solace, to help and to heal
The sick world that leans on her. This was Lucille.*

* (Sister Seraphine.)

[137]

COME PENSIVE NUN
From Il Penseroso

JOHN MILTON

Come pensive Nun, devout and pure,
Sober, steadfast, and demure,
All in a robe of darkest grain,
Flowing with majestic train,
And sable stole of cyprus lawn
Over thy decent shoulders drawn.
Come; but keep thy wonted state,
With even step, and musing gait,
And looks commercing with the skies,
Thy wrapt soul sitting in thine eyes.

A FRENCH NUN

Dinah Maria Mulock

She sits upon her pallet bed;
  Her heavy eyes down bending lowly,
Sad thoughts may rack her weary head,
  But never thoughts unholy:
And though she murmurs Latin prayers,
To say she prays not — who dares?

She has no husband and no child,
  Is half forgot by mother, father:
Yet won by her sweet aspect mild,
  Round her the convent scholars gather,
Though shut is every kindred door,
She is the sister of the poor.

We serve not as she serves — good sooth!
  We live not as she lives — half dying;
We think our truth the only truth
  But God forbid we call hers lying;
Or doubt that Mary's holy Son
Has comfort for the lonely nun.

THE WHITE VEIL

Grace Fallow Norton

I have forgot them all.
The faces of my friends.
I hear the shepherds call,
I watch the fountain fall,
And there remembrance ends.

For now no heart I have,
Only a scarlet flower,
Only a silver wave —
For these my heart I gave,
And for a rainbow shower!

And late within this land
I have become the bride
Of him within whose hand
Rests the wild silent strand,
The sombre mountain-side.

A silence full of song —
His shadow full of light . . .
Long I desired him, long,
Following amid the throng
Ever his mantle white.

And now his veil I wear,
Lord of sorrows that cease.
His veil is white and fair,
Woven of evening air —
O white veil of Peace.

A NUN*

Christina Georgina Rossetti

My heart is as a freeborn bird
   Caged in my cruel breast,
That flutters, flutters evermore,
   Nor sings nor is at rest,
But beats against the prison bars,
   As knowing its own nest
Far off beyond the clouded west.

My soul is as a hidden fount
   Shut in by clammy clay
That struggles with an upward moan,
   Striving to force its way
Up through the turf, over the grass,
   Up up into the day
Where twilight no more turneth grey.

Oh for the grapes of the True Vine
   Growing in Paradise,
Whose tendrils join the Tree of Life
   To that which maketh wise —
Growing beside the Living Well
   Whose sweetest waters rise
Where tears are wiped from tearful eyes!

* This is the third of three poems written under the title "Three Nuns."
The united poem was inserted into the prose tale *Maud* with the
observation, "Pray read the mottoes; put together they form a most
exquisite little song which the nuns sing in Italy." This little song has
been translated by the poet's brother, William Michael Rossetti: "The
heart sighs and I know not wherefore. It may be sighing for love but to
me it says not so. Answer me, my heart, wherefore sighest thou? It
answers: I want God — I sigh for Jesus."

Editor

Oh for the waters of that Well
    Round which the Angels stand —
Oh for the Shadow of the Rock
    On my heart's weary land —
Oh for the Voice to guide me when
    I turn to either hand,
Guiding me till I reach heaven's strand!

Thou world from which I am come out,
    Keep all thy gems and gold;
Keep thy delights and precious things,
    Thou that art waxing old.
My heart shall beat with a new life
    When thine is dead and cold;
When thou dost fear I shall be bold.

When Earth shall pass away with all
    Her pride and pomp of sin,
The City builded without hands
    Shall safely shut me in.
All the rest is but vanity
    Which others strive to win:
Where their hopes end my joys begin.

I will not look upon a rose
    Though it is fair to see:
The flowers planted in Paradise
    Are budding now for me:
Red roses like love visible
    Are blowing on their tree,
Or white like virgin purity.

I will not look unto the sun
  Which setteth night by night:
In the untrodden courts of heaven
  My crown shall be more bright.
Lo! in the New Jerusalem
  Founded and built aright
My very feet shall tread on light.

With foolish riches of this world
  I have bought treasure where
Nought perisheth: for this white veil
  I gave my golden hair;
I gave the beauty of my face
  For vigils, fasts, and prayer;
I gave all for this cross I bear.

My heart trembled when first I took
  The vows which must be kept.
At first it was a weariness
  To watch when once I slept:
The path was rough and sharp with thorns;
  My feet bled as I stept;
The cross was heavy and I wept.

While still the names rang in mine ear
  Of daughter, sister, wife,
The outside world still looked so fair
  To my weak eyes, and rife
With beauty, my heart almost failed;
  Then in the desperate strife
I prayed, as one who prays for life —

Until I grew to love what once
　　Had been so burdensome.
So now, when I am faint because
　　Hope deferred seems to numb
My heart, I yet can plead and say,
　　Although my lips are dumb —
The Spirit and the Bride say, Come.

A SISTER OF CHARITY *

FREDERICK G. SCOTT

She made a nunnery of her life
  Plain duties hedged it round,
No echoes of the outer strife
  Could reach its hallowed ground.

Her rule was simple as her creed,
  She tried to do each day
Some act of kindness that might speed
  A sad soul on its way.

She had no wealth, and yet she made
  So many rich at heart;
Her lot was hidden, yet she played
  No inconspicuous part.

Some wondered men had passed her by,
  Some said she would not wed,
I think the secret truth must lie
  Long buried with the dead.

That cheery smile, that gentle touch
  That heart so free from stain,
Could have no other source but such
  As lies in conquered pain.

* This "Sister of Charity" was a devout, charitable Protestant lady, but the verse is included in this Anthology because it is truly a high tribute to our sisters that its author, an English Protestant clergyman, should compare her life and works to those of a Sister of Charity.

Editor

All living creatures loved her well,
   And blessed the ground she trod:
The pencillings on her Bible tell
   Her communing with God.

And when the call came suddenly
   And sleep preceded death,
There was no struggle we could see,
   No hard and labored breath.

Gentle as dawn the end drew nigh;
   Her life had been so sweet,
I think she did not need to die
   To reach the Master's feet.

THE ABBESS
Marmion, Canto Second

SIR WALTER SCOTT

The Abbess was of noble blood,
But early took the veil and hood,
Ere upon life she cast a look,
Or knew the world that she foresook.
Fair too was she, and kind had been
As she was fair, but ne'er had seen
For her a timid lover sigh,
Nor knew the influence of her eye.
Love, to her ear, was but a name
Combined with vanity and shame;
Her hopes, her fears, her joys, were all
Bounded within the cloister wall:
The deadliest sin her mind could reach,
Was of monastic rule the breach;
And her ambition's highest aim
To emulate Saint Hilda's fame.
For this she gave her ample dower,
To raise the convent's eastern tower;
For this, with carving, rare and quaint,
She deck'd the chapel of the saint,
And gave the relic-shrine of cost,
With ivory and gems emboss'd.
The poor her Convent's bounty blest,
The pilgrim in its hall found rest.

Black was her garb, her rigid rule
Reformed on Benedictine school;
Her cheek was pale, her form was spare;

Vigils, and penances austere,
Had early quenched the light of youth.
But gentle was the dame, in sooth:
Though vain of her religious sway,
She loved to see her maids obey,
Yet nothing stern was she in cell,
And the nuns loved their Abbess well.

A NOVICE
Measure For Measure Act I, 5

WILLIAM SHAKESPEARE*

Lucio to Isabella

Hail Virgin, if you be, as these cheek-roses
Proclaim you are no less!.
I hold you as a thing ensky'd and sainted,
By your renouncement an immortal spirit,
And to be talked with in sincerity
As with a saint.

---

* Shakespeare is not placed among the Catholic poets because the evidence of his Catholicity is merely, no matter how strongly, presumptive. In an age when it was popular to write disparagingly of popery, not one of his works contains the slightest reflection on the Catholic Church, or on any of its practices. Nor do we find any eulogy on the Reformation. His panegyric on Queen Elizabeth is cautiously expressed, while Queen Katherine, the Catholic wife of Henry VIII, is placed in a state of veneration. Isabella, to whom our quotation was addressed, was a conventual novice and is exhibited as a lovely example of female purity. It is an undisputed fact that the father of the poet lived and died in communion with the Catholic Church and that his sister was a nun at Wroxall, until the forced dissolution of the Convent. She died at Stratford when Shakespeare was fourteen years old and certainly must have influenced his childhood. His grammar school teacher Simon Hunt, was a devout Catholic.

Editor

THE NUN

Odell Shepard

One glance and I had lost her in the riot
    Of tangled cries.
She trod the clamor with a cloistral quiet
    Deep in her eyes:
As though she heard the muted music only
    That silence makes
Amid dim mountain summits and on lonely
    Deserted lakes.

There is some broken song her heart remembers
    From long ago,
Some love lies buried deep, some passion's embers
    Smothered in snow,
Far voices of a joy that sought and missed her
    Fail now and cease,
And this has given to the deep eyes of God's sister
    Their dreadful peace.

A BEGGAR FOR GOD[*]

John Stigall

She stands in rusty black upon the curb
Her begging basket in her broad veined hand,
She has foregone a pride that could disturb
The modest sweetness of her mute demand.

Her face is blunt and plain, and many years
Have killed the freshness of her distant spring;
But in this silent aging nun appears
A tempered strength that only love can bring.

She has endured beyond the edge of pain —
Her eyes have seen and she has understood
That men are wanton children who have slain
Their heart's deep love and then have called it good.

And she has learned in silence from her God
That man's chameleon heart demands the price
She pays. Her patient swollen feet have trod
Christ's holy road — the way of sacrifice.

And hers is peace that nothing can disturb
The modest sweetness in her mute demand.
She stands in rusty black upon the curb
Her begging basket in her broad veined hand.

[*] A Little Sister of the Poor.

A QUEEN BECOMES AN ABBESS [1]

ALFRED LORD TENNYSON [2]

Queen Guinevere had fled the court, and sat
There in the holy house of Almesbury
Weeping, none with her save a little maid,
A novice; one low light betwixt them burned
Blurred by the creeping mist, for all abroad,
Beneath a moon unseen albeit at full,
The white mist, like a face-cloth to the face,
Clung to the dead earth, and the land was still. . . .

                      She looked and saw
The novice weeping, suppliant, and said to her,
"Yea, little maid, for am I not forgiven?"
Then looking up beheld the holy nuns
All round her, weeping; and her heart was loosed
Within her, and she wept with these and said,
"O shut me round with narrowing nunnery-walls,
Meek maidens, from the voices crying 'Shame'. . . .
So let me, if you do not shudder at me,
Nor shun to call me sister, dwell with you;
Wear black and white and be a nun like you,
Fast with your fasts, not feasting with your feasts;
Grieve with your griefs, not grieving at your joys,
But not rejoicing; mingle with your rites;

---

[1] Saint Mary Magdalene's repentance and her great love for Christ
made her worthy to become the friend of Jesus and the companion of
Mary Immaculate. Likewise Queen Guinevere's repentance and her
new found love for Christ, made her pure enough to become the com
panion of the nuns of Almesbury, and eventually their Abbess.

                      Editc

[2] *The Idylls of the King* — "Guinevere"

Pray and be prayed for; lie before your shrines;
Do each low office of your holy house;
Walk your dim cloister, and distribute dole
To poor sick people, richer in His eyes
Who ransomed us and haler too than I:
And treat their loathsome hurts and heal mine own;
And so wear out in almsdeeds and in prayer
The sombre close of that voluptuous day
Which wrought the ruin of my lord the King."

She said: they took her to themselves; and she
Still hoping, fearing "is it yet too late?"
Dwelt with them, till in time their Abbess died.
Then she for her good deeds and her pure life,
And for the power of ministration in her,
And likewise for the high rank she had borne,
Was chosen Abbess, there an Abbess lived
For three brief years, there an Abbess passed
To where beyond these voices there is peace.

SISTER MARY VERONICA

Nancy Byrd Turner

The soft-shod nuns have laid the last fold straight
In her last raiment, telling their slow beads
With measured memories of her faithful deeds,
And prayers for her soul's sake, importunate.
Now they are gone, grey shadows, to the call
Of a far vesper bell. At foot and head,
  Two pallid tapers tall —
Glimmering, gaunt, thick stifled with the gloom
Of wan dusk deep'ning in the naked room —
  Guard her, a short day dead.

White and austere and virginal she lies:
Pale brow, pale fallen lids, hair meetly drest;
Straight shoulders never burdened, mother-wise,
Of weary little bodies sleep-possest;
Meek mouth uncurved of kisses, folded eyes;
Thin hands light linked across a shallow breast;
Beyond desire, past sorrow and past surprise,
  Mute, passionless, at rest.

Strange, as I watch, a faint soft flame of youth
Brightens upon her, slowly, wondrously,
  And lends her magic dower —
A look of vision and of prophecy.
Not curve of cheek and color of fine rose,
Not curl nor fleeting dimple — none of these,
But the warm beauty and the tender ruth
Of April sunlight on an autumn flower
  One brief miraculous hour.

Lo, what at last are dust and age and death!
Time can not touch the innermost spirit —— See —
Half smiling, confident of joy to be,
Sure of her heritage, with bated breath
    Biding her destiny
She waits, a slim girl wistful of the truth,
Life still a dream — Love still a mystery!

FRIDAY NIGHT*

Evelyn Underhill

Must I take
The scourge in hand for Jesu's sake?
Kneel and cry
"Mercy, mercy! God most high."

Lord, I quail
At the Miserere's wail,
Yet I know
Love should joy to suffer so.

Give me grace
And courage for a little space.
Loving Thee
So to bear love's penalty.

For the blame
Of all who mock Thy holy name
I would give
This my flesh, that they may live.

For the wrong
Wrought by evil wills and strong,
Take the price
Of my body's sacrifice.

* In a foreword to this poem the author writes: "In certain convents, on
every Friday night, the nuns scourge themselves, each in her own cell,
with the door open upon the corridor. A verse of the *Miserere* is intoned
between each stripe." — In convents where this practice is allowed, great
care is exercised that it does not degenerate into fanaticism. The body
may be scourged to inflict pain, but not to the extent that the health is
injured.

Editor

Take my all!
Hold my heart and soul in thrall!
    Thou canst not
Take the splendor of my lot.

    To the crash
Of the slow-descending lash
    As I bow,
Lo! I am Thy partner now.

    I am found
With Thee at the pillar bound.
    I have worn
Bitter crown of budding thorn.

    Yea! a part
Of Thy dread atoning art,
    Never done,
Is the penance of a nun.

    Holy pain!
Smite, ah! smite me once again.
    Precious blood!
Add my drop to Thy great flood.

    — What is this?
Shall I dare to ask my bliss
    In the grief
He endures for our relief?

    Shall I dare
Claim the right of entrance there
    Where alone
God doth for the world atone?

'Twas in pride
Angels from His vision died;
    And shall I
Set my little hurt so high?

    So I kneel
Full of wounds Thy stripes shall heal.
    Holy pain!
Make me, make me whole again!

    First to dread,
Now to shame have I been led:
    Lord, I pray,
Purge the smears of self away.

    By this smart
Shatter and remake my heart;
    Snatch my love
From the coils that pride hath wove.

    'Stablish me
In Thy Spirit strong and free;
    Let the voice
Thou hast quenched, again rejoice.

    In Thy sight
Shining with a sacred light,
    Only then
Shall my wounds avail for men.

COR CORDIUM *

Wilbur Underwood

I

Heart of hearts — I whisper this for name,
  So far above all other loves thou art;
Dear head, to me sun-crowned with living flame,
  Sole sun in that dim way I walk apart;
Christ's wounds were not more surely burned nor deep
  In Francis' stainless hands, than on my soul
Is set the imprint of thy love, to keep
  My straying feet from many a dreaded goal;
Do I but see thy face the deadening bands
  Are loosed, and I can look upon the skies;
If thou but fold my hands in thy dear hands
  The joy of earth laughs in my weary eyes,
Thy ocean life sweeps o'er the barrier sands
  And gulfs them — and my spirit seaward flies.

II

I may not even touch my desolate hands
  To your dear hands — nor look upon your face;
God's angel like a golden shadow stands
  Us two between — and all that solemn space
Is silent with the awe of cherubim
  Who brood upon love's new Gethsemane;
Though God should speak — I think I could not see,
  Heaven's paths seem far away and cold and dim;

* For one who refused the love of man in order to give her heart to God
in the cloister.

Editor

[159]

I have no wish in Paradisal skies
    To know the phantom joying of the dead;
My utter need is your dear human eyes,
    The human rapture of so dear a head
That turns toward me — there just beyond where lies
    The shadow of that veiléd shape of dread.

THE WHITE SISTERS OF CULION

Wilbur Underwood

The Bridegroom calls and led by love they go
Even where on barren mount in burning seas
Earth casts her leper-plagued to rot alone
Where heat and horror fight for masteries.

They bear, these humble nuns, a load we shun;
White, white like their white Christ, transfiguréd
Strong with the love that conquered death and hell
They move consoling midst the living dead.

O narrowing self, does not their sacrifice
Condemn your meanness more than Judgment Day?
Christ's way is service; turn, stretch forth your hand
Unto the nearer need and find the Way.

THE FEMALE MARTYR *

John Greenleaf Whittier

"Bring out your dead!" The midnight street
   Heard and gave back the low, hoarse call;
Harsh fell the thread of hasty feet —
Glanced through the dark the coarse white sheet —
   Her coffin and her pall.
   "What — only one!" the brutal hackman said,
As, with an oath, he spurned away the dead.

How sunk the inmost hearts of all
   As rolled the dead cart slowly by,
With creeking wheel and harsh hoof-fall!
The dying turned him to the wall,
   To hear it and to die!
Onward it rolled; while oft its driver stayed,
And hoarsely clamored, "Ho! — bring out your dead."

It paused beside the burial place;
   "Toss in your load!" and it was done. —
With quick hand and averted face,
Hastily to the grave's embrace
   They cast them one by one —
Stranger and friend — the evil and the just,
   Together trodden in the churchyard dust!

---

* Mary G. —, aged eighteen, a Sister of Charity, died in one of our
Atlantic cities, during the prevalence of the Indian cholera, while in
voluntary attendance upon the sick.

                  Author's Note

And thou, young martyr! — thou wast there —
   No white-robed sisters round thee trod —
Nor holy hymn, nor funeral prayer
Rose through the damp and noisome air,
   Giving thee to thy God;
Nor flower, nor cross, nor hallowed taper gave
Grace to the dead, and beauty to the grave!

Yet, gentle sufferer! there shall be
   In every heart of kindly feeling,
A rite as holy paid to thee
As if beneath the convent-tree
   Thy sisterhood were kneeling,
At vesper hours, like sorrowing angels keeping,
Their tearful watch around thy place of sleeping.

For thou wast one in whom the light
   Of Heaven's own love was kindled well.
Enduring with a martyr's might,
Through weary day and wakeful night
   Far more than words may tell:
Gentle, and meek, and lonely, and unknown —
Thy mercies measured by thy God alone!

Where many hearts were failing — where
   The throngful street grew foul with death,
O high-souled martyr! thou wast there,
Inhaling from the loathsome air
Poison with every breath.
   Yet shrinking not from offices of dread
For the wrung dying and the unconscious dead.

And where the sickly taper shed
    Its light through vapors, damp, confined,
Hushed as a seraph's fell thy tread —
A new Electra by the bed
    Of suffering human kind!
Pointing the spirit in its dark dismay,
To that pure hope which fadeth not away.

Innocent teacher of the high
    And holy mysteries of Heaven!
How turned to thee each glazing eye,
In mute and awful sympathy,
    As thy low prayers were given;
And the o'er hovering Spoiler wore, the while,
An angel's features — a deliverer's smile!

A blessed task! — and worthy one
    Who, turning from the world, as thou,
Before life's pathway had begun
To leave its spring-time flower and sun,
    Had sealed her early vow;
Giving to God her beauty and her youth,
Her pure affections and her guileless truth.

Earth may not claim thee. Nothing here
    Could be for thee a meet reward;
Thine is a treasure far more dear —
Eye hath not seen it, nor the ear
    Of living mortal heard —
The joys prepared — the promised bliss above —
The holy presence of Eternal love!

Sleep on in peace. The earth has not
   A nobler name than thine shall be.
The deeds by martial manhood wrought,
The lofty energies of thought,
   The fire of poesy —
These have but frail and fading honors; — thine
Shall Time unto Eternity consign.

Yea, and when thrones shall crumble down,
   And human pride and grandeur fall—
The herald's line of long renown—
The mitre and the kingly crown—
   Perishing glories all!
The pure devotion of thy generous heart
Shall live in heaven, of which it was a part.

III

POEMS BY NUNS ABOUT NUNS

LAUGHTER IN HEAVEN
In Memory of a School Sister of Notre Dame

SISTER MARY ANGELINE, S.S.N.D.

Laughter in Heaven? Then I shall surely find you
After this prisoned spirit is set free,
After the wick of every shining candle
Is snuffed in earth's dim caravansary.

For song was on your lips and joy around you,
Shod with the stars, walking a country lane.
Now you are dead, and your remembered laughter
I can not hear for the insistent rain.

IMPRESS OF THE CRUCIFIX

On the Heart of Saint Clare of Monte Falce, an Augustinian Nun

MOTHER MARY ALPHONSA, O.S.D.*

From her willing heart He hewed Him a Cross. (My heart,
How it flees the shadow of pain.) Fashioned the nails
   And the scourge and the spear, and a Crown of Thorns
      made part
Of her flesh. (My flesh, how it shrinks when suffering assails.)

With each throb of her love, each sigh, each prayer He
      wrought
Till His Sacred Form took shape. (How little the space
   In my life where God may work.) and His coming brought
The whiteness of pain, the stillness of peace to her face.

Nor the world did dream her myst'ried part till the veil
Of silence was pierced by death. (My lips, how they speak
In meaningless words each trial; my lips, how they fail
God's love.) Ah, Martyr-Saint, my love is weak —

---

* Mother Alphonsa (Rose Hawthorne) was the daughter of Nathaniel
Hawthorne the well known American author. With her husband,
George Parsons Lathrop, she joined the Catholic Church, and after
his death she became a nun in the Servants of Relief (Sisters of St.
Dominic) a congregation which she established for the care of poor
cancer patients. From two small rooms and one patient in the most
dreary part of New York's East End, her work has grown until today
it is carried on in commodious and modern buildings in New York,
Philadelphia, Fall River and Atlanta. No remuneration is received from
patients and there is no reserve fund. Its success has been remarkable
because the Sisters depend upon the goodness of God, and the benevo-
lence of the public, and have no other protection against bankruptcy
and defeat.

Editor

Too weak to ask that He hew Him a Cross: hew
From its living depths; too frail to seek a share
In pain, and bitter its loss that it can not sue
For an anguished hour — that it fails such love to dare

PERPETUAL VOWS

Sister Mary Angelita, B.V.M.

Before the earth with glittering seas was girded,
    Before the starry lamps were touched to flame,
Before the shining hosts of heaven were marshalled,
    God thought of thee and called thee by thy name.

This is the hour on which His gaze was centered,
    In far-off dim eternities sublime,
When He decreed to call thee forth from nothing
    And set thee on the shores of life and time.

His yearning love o'er leaped the mighty chasm
    Of centuries that still must rise and fall
Ere thou shouldst come to Him, thy royal Lover,
    And plight thy troth and yield to Him thine all.

O happy Christ, Who on Thy little creature
    Dost set Thy heart, Thou art content today!
O happy bride, who canst with such slight dower
    The treasures of eternal love repay.

THE NUN'S HEART

Anonymous

Ah! make a shady garden of my heart
  With silence safely walléd in,
Then from the cruel world of sin
  Come, Thou, from out the crowd and rest apart.

May my desires be dew-wet verdant grass
  To bring refreshment to Thy aching feet,
And though no flowers Thine eyes may greet
  They will spring up, dear Lord, as Thou dost pass.

Oh! bid the desert blossom forth the rose,
  The flower of love for Thee alone to wear,
Though others may its fragrant perfume share
  To make life sweeter: still for Thee it grows.

May violets of a lowly humble mind
  Be trodden by thee closer to the ground,
So that their perfume may alone be found
  And all the balmy air grow still more kind.

Thou must be Gardener, Lord, as well as Guest:
  Train all my flowers to follow Thy sweet will,
Guard them from aught that might their beauty kill.
  Then come from out the sinning world and rest.

THE CONTEMPLATIVE

Sister Mary Benvenuta, O.P.

Why should she wait Death's bidding to begin
What she was made of? God had set her place
Before the hidden beauty of His Face.
She anchoress, to angels made akin,
By walls of prayer, shuts out Time's fretful din,
Nor needs him save to bid him run apace
And bring kind Death, who, in a little space,
Shall draw faith's curtain and let sunshine in.

Yet in the darkness fragrant as a night
In summer, murmurous with mystery
Her lips grope for God's feet, and when the light
Floods in, she will not need to stir, for He
Her heaven is here, Whom henceforth she shall see,
With satiate, yet never tiring sight.

CLOISTER

Mother Mary Campion, S.H.J.C.

Earth-lover that I am, you say,
For convent walls I squandered in a day,
The beauty that a God
Had meant for me:
The rising surge of strong, majestic hills,
The poignant calm of seas with cool rain stilled,
The sobbing of stabbed autumn
Bleeding itself away.
Never for me the music of the elves,
Played on gossamer strings within the dells
That harbor pools so deep,
So still, so cool.

But now a deeper beauty do I know:
The rising surge of chant, majestic, slow,
The calm serenity of lives
Avowed to pain.
This deeper beauty brings me close to tears,
To tears and God. It stills my very fears
To hear an organ sob
The "Agnus Dei."
In children I find my every need
Of Elfin music. In their eyes lurk indeed
The dancing imp of mischief
Gossamer-tied.
Deep beauty. For small sacrifice I sow
A whiter harvest. O God, may I too know
The depthless pools of peace
In an old nun's eyes.

THE DAY OF MY PROFESSION

Sister Mary Christina, S.H.C.J. *

When men describe a happy lot
   'Tis peace or joy that they portray,
But these sweet words they render not
   What God has given to thee to-day.

Men can describe what men can give,
   But what our God reserves for those
Who come within His courts to live,
   Its heavenly name no mortal knows.

The brightest joy is dull to this,
   The deepest peace to this, unrest;
The memory of eternal bliss
   Has dawned this day within thy breast —

Has dawned, and every day will shine
   More brightly than the day before,
Till thy Beloved shall be thine
   And thou be His forevermore.

---

* Sister Mary Christina was the eldest daughter of Coventry Patmore, the poet who has so beautifully and so well devoted his genius to the glorification of conjugal love. Because the Church so highly honors the virginal state, it must not be concluded that she does not respect the holy state of matrimony. With Saint Paul she compares the union of a Christian man and his wife to the union of Christ and the Church. It is worthy of remark that the only poets of importance who have sung almost exclusively of conjugal love are Catholics — William Habington and Coventry Patmore.

Editor

IDEAL
Ann — Who Became a Nun

Sister Miriam Clare, O.S.F.
(*A Sister of St. Francis of Joliet, Ill.*)

You love the mountain tops; you lift your face
Up to the stars and walk above the clouds;
I scorn low lands. You wrap Pain in a smile
And wear her as a glowing brooch beneath
Your scapular and pressed against your heart;
I try to clasp it too. You stoop to hunt
Out each low thing — retiring violets
Or lilies-of-the-vale; I never glance
At flaunting, showy hollyhocks — or phlox.

Your eyes are flecked with childhood, shining bits
Of everlasting childhood, learned beside
A crib where Childhood lay; I kneel there too.

You lean your head against a nail-pierced Hand
And glory in the Blood that stains your cheek;
And I — all trembling — striving ever in
Your steps — lift up my face presumptuously.

PRAYER FOR A SILVER JUBILEE

SISTER MARY COLMAN, S.S.N.D.

Dear Lord, it's but a silver chain,
Its links are small.
I've labored all these years
To fashion it.
You see, it is not beautiful at all.
"Not beautiful, My spouse?"
A soft response
From Christ, Lover Divine.
"I treasure little things, you know.
Its links are exquisitely fine.
The hidden years that form the chain,
Each deed performed, each step you took,
Each tiny thought you lifted up to Me —
These are the links of silver
In your chain,
Most beautiful to see.
And in exchange?
Ah! that is a secret between your heart and Mine.
Come, spouse of My Heart, accept My gift,
My Love Divine."

VOCATION

Sister Mary David
(*A Sister of Mercy of Manchester, N. H.*)

She walked with God upon a golden morn
    And listened to a thrush's love sweet call,
But though her heart was filled with joyous song,
    She never knew she walked with God at all.

She strayed with Him down long blue afternoons
    Among tall trees where tranquil shadows pass,
And when she stopped to court forbidden dreams
    She heard His garments rustling in the grass.

Then when the violet dusk fell softly down
    And mesmerized the world with potent charms,
With mighty passion purer than the light
    He swept her upward in His yearning arms.

All that she cherished — dreams and youth and self
    Was burned and purged with love's divinest breath
And hearts uncomprehending deemed her mad
    Who fell in love with pain, contempt and death.

EXCHANGE

Sister Mary Dorothy Ann, C.S.C.

I am all Thine, Beloved, for
I come
Unbound and free;
Now I am stripped of everything
I love,
To love but Thee;
Of everything, and yet my Lord
I have fair memory.

The wide world is my home; but once
I knew
A garden close,
And sheltering walls encircled by
The press
Of rambling roses.
In every soul that I may help
My heart
A new home knows.
And once when all my life was young
I dreamt
Of little feet,
And tiny hands and rosy mouth;
Ah, Lord,
Those dreams were sweet!
To-day a thousand little hands
Await
My love to meet.

And in the dream of yesterday,
The whole
Wide world was mine.
I held it close against my heart;
But now
A Love divine
Has given more than life can give,
Himself,
The Bread and Wine.

FOR A NOVICE

SISTER MARY EDWARDINE
(*A Sister of Mercy of Grand Rapids, Mich.*)

I have prayed for you, prayed that your path may be
Never content, that you may never rest
Where languid shadows fall,
Missing the sweet compulsion of His breast.

I have prayed always that thirst be your guest,
And hunger be the board whereat you dine,
That you may find Him all,
Who would Himself be both your Bread and Wine.

I pray the white stars ever may not shine
Through the long night that you must tread alone,
Fearful you might not see
The luminous Feet that walk beside your own.

[178]

THE SOLDIER AND THE NUN

Sister Mary Eleanore, C.S.C.

So madly noisy are men's battle ways —
He was worn out with noise.
                         His troubled gaze,
Troubled with death, found her, and suddenly
A hope, new born was his. So quietly
She knelt.
           He hated noise, noise that with pain
Had blasted him. The noise of praise, how vain
It seemed — yet it had been so fine to hear
When he marched forth, "For God and country dear."

Then fear laid hold of him. This awful death
That fought him, fought him for his very breath!
Anguish grew in his gaze.
                          How patiently
Her lips were praying. Strange — what was it she
Had said?
          This his last battle she would share
And fight, not death, sure victor, but despair
That now was taunting him with every sin.

How brave she looked — he felt that she could win
Their fight. Her path of glory was, she said,
Like his, of sacrifice, and duty led
Her way!
         Peace slipped into his dying gaze —
So sweetly quiet are God's battle ways.

THE WORLD TO ANY NUN

Sister Mary Eleanore, C.S.C.

Yours are the tranquil ways
Of lily boats on shadowed pools;
Waves do not beat through nights and days
Your prow with force made cruel
By scourging winds that do not sleep;
The sun that pitilessly smites
The ships upon the deep
Is filtered into tender lights
Upon your quiet boat;
The surge that deafens with its roar,
Dissolves to silver note on note
About your placid shore.
And I, who scorn your tempered ways
When proudly I ride by,
My face young in the sunlit haze,
My sails upstanding white and high,
Go questing far for golden sands,
For power and flaming love.
But I can never reach those lands,
The storm will sometime break above
My boat and blast its strength.
Peace does not dwell upon the deep;
The battered ship must turn at length
To surcease harbors keep.
When that hour comes, as come it must,
Then from the darkness I shall cry
To you: "I am your trust;
You have a part with the Most High
To share in saving me.

Reach out your hands with kindness blessed
To draw my boat from out this sea
Into your place of rest."

CONVENT MORNING

Sister Mary Eugene, S.S.N.D.

She could not sleep all night for happiness.
      The clock within the tower
      Loudly told off each hour
With lengthening stress.
      One, two, three, four—
      Just one hour more,
And dawn would usher in her bridal day.
Laid out in trim array,
      Her wedding gown and veil.
      Nor did she fail
Of ornament. A string of beads, a ring ——
To her strong Lover will she bring
      A gift; priceless 'twill be ——
      The chaliced beauty of her chastity.

And He, her Spouse, was waiting through the night,
Waiting within the glow of crimson light,
      For her swift footfall
      Coming down the hall.
Lo! here she comes! Her fair young face
Coifed in the glow of grace.
      The lines of her black gown
      Fall gracefully down
To her all-eager feet.
There at the altar rail they meet—
Lover and loved one. The eternal vows, the kiss,
The mystic feast of bliss—

She His; He hers!
Whatever else occurs
Has naught in it of mutability.

Than earthly love, no human bond is stronger:
But this is heavenly love. Eternity is longer.

MAUREEN O'REILLY

Sister Mary Eugene, S.S.N.D.

Did you know Maureen O'Reilly? She was lovely as the
    morning,
  All the color of the Maytime was reflected in her face.
Raven hair, and eyes of azure, with a glint of Celtic in them,
  Lent an extra touch of beauty to her simple, girlish grace.

There was zest and gladness in her; health and buoyancy of
    spirit,
  With a charming bit of shyness and of maidenly restraint.
Just to catch her rapt expression as she came back from
    Communion,
  Made one feel her heart was pulsing with the ardor of a
    saint.

She could wield a tennis racquet best of all her clever com-
    rades,
  She was expert with a mashie, and in hockey was a star.
She was captain of the basket-ball, and led her team to vic-
    tory,
  But was modest in her leadership as all true leaders are.

She was quick at writing verses; she was interested in science;
  She could sing a classic aria in cadence clear and high.
She could trip the light fantastic in a truly fairy fashion,
  "And a' the lads they smiled at her when comin' through
    the rye."

But she cared not for their glances, and the flattering tributes
    paid her,

She accepted them in friendship and enjoyed their boyish
     fun.
The white secret of her winsomeness this morning broke
     upon us,
When she left us brokenhearted and ran off to be a nun.

A NUN'S BELOVED

Mother Francis Raphael, O.S.D.*

Mountains that upwards to the clouds arise,
    Odorous with thyme whereon the wild bees linger,
Jewelled with flowers of a thousand dyes,
    Their petals tinted by no mortal finger:
How solemn in their grey old age they stand,
    Hills piled on hills in silent majesty,
Lofty and strong and beautiful and grand,
    All this and more is my Belovéd to me.

Come forth into the woods — in yonder valley
    Where rippling waters murmur through the glade,
There 'neath the rustling boughs of some green alley
    We'll watch the golden light and quivering shade;
Or couched on mossy banks we'll lie and listen
    To song birds pouring forth their vernal glee.
Wave on ye woods, ye fairy fountains glisten,
    But more, far more is my Belovéd to me.

Know ye the land where fragrant winds awaken
    In spicy forests hidden from the eye,
Where richest perfumes from the boughs are shaken,
    And flowers unnoticed blush and bloom and die;

* A member of the High Church party in the Church of England, Augusta Theodosia Drane made a plan for a religious order of Anglican women. When a distinguished Anglican rector told her that an order such as she had outlined was already in existence in the Catholic Church, she began an examination of the Catholic claims, and from the Church of England went over to the Church in England, and eventually, as Mother Francis Raphael, became the prioress-provincial of the English Dominican Sisters.

Editor's Note

Sweet is the eternal spring that there reposes
    On wondrous isles that gem the sunny sea,
And sweet the gales that breathe o'er beds of roses,
    But sweeter far is my Belovéd to me.

A gentle sound wakes in the hush of even,
    The whisper of a light and cooling breeze,
It stirs when twilight shades are in the heaven,
    And bows the tufted foliage of the trees;
It fans my cheek, its music softly stealing
    Speaks to my heart in loving mystery,
Ah, gentle breeze full well thou art revealing
    The joy that my Belovéd is to me.

Yea all the fairest forms that nature scatters,
    And all melodious sounds that greet the ear,
The murmuring music of the running waters,
    The golden harvest fields that crown the year,
The crimson morn, the calm and dewy even,
    The tranquil moonlight on the slumbering sea,
All are but shadows, forms of beauty given
    To tell what my Belovéd is to me.

THE DIVINE CALL
"The Master has come and calleth for thee."—St. John XI, 28.

SISTER MARY GENEVIEVE
(*A Sister of Providence of St. Mary of the Woods*)

The Master calls for thee.
Arise my soul and hasten to His feet,
Thy sorrow like the morning mist will flee
There in His presence sweet.

'Tis He, thine only Lord,
He loving comes to be thine humble guest,
"Come unto Me"—His sweet consoling word,
"And I will give thee rest."

'Tis He, thy faithful Friend
Who longs to fold thee to His Heart Divine,
Who in His love would share unto the end
Each joy and grief of thine.

'Tis He, thy Love: no more
O soul of mine, resist thy heavenly Spouse.
In grateful love, go plight Him o'er and o'er
Thine everlasting vows.

Go, sit thou at His feet
And ponder o'er the lesson of His Heart.
Go, spend thy life in one Communion sweet,
Go choose the better part.

✿   ✿   ✿

I'm Thine, dear Lord, forever more
  Whatever may befall,
And Thou art mine, my Life, my Love,
  My Jesus and my All.

ON A CERTAIN NUN

SISTER MARY IGNATIUS
(*A Sister of St. Joseph of Brooklyn, N. Y.*)

I met her on the poetry page
  A disembodied cry
Of certitude uncircumscribed—
  I passed her quickly by.

I did not want to know her age
  Or if she's short or tall
Or if she teaches high or low
  Or any grade at all . . .

I love her nebulosity
  Because it keeps me staring
At one triumphant thought of hers
  And not at what she's wearing—

I love her anonymity
  Because it leaves me power
To build the garden of herself
  From one essential flower.

LETTER FROM A POSTULANT

Sister Mary Irma, B.V.M.

Through all the days of your secret, wishful planning
  My ears were keyed to the wind in the locust tree.
I turned, transpierced, at the sudden breaking of blossoms,
  Unneedful of man as the inviolate sea.

How should I know that you saw not the almond blossoms
  For the dark cascades of my hair as I bent above?
How should I hear, for the voice of the Bridegroom calling,
  The muted strains of an earth-encompassed love?

Only the loneliness surging to wind-swept horizons
  Could answer the loneliness there in my heart that beat;
Only all-giving to ultimate All could supply me,
  Only the vastness of God could give roads to my feet.

And you, whose joy would have been in a homely garden,
  Watching the butterflies circling about my head,
For the gift you have given in silence, shall share all my
      heaven;
  While you grieve for the stone I denied you, I knead for
      you Bread.

A SISTER LIGHTS THE CANDLES

Sister Mary Jeremy, O.P.
(*A Dominican Sister of Sinsinawa, Wis.*)

Dahlia-red, the shadowed curtains
   Moved in the dusk and she came through
Holding a simpler rod than Aaron's
   Wherefrom a subtler wonder grew;

For every ivory stem she crowned with
   Fabulous bursts of daisy flame
Bright in the stillness, point and petal,
   How fast that angels' Maytime came!

Her leafless, scentless, birdless orchard
   Touched walls and roof till they were air,
Blued into mist and clean forgotten.
   The winds of peace flowed everywhere.

Still in the midst the blowing fires
   In rows and slants were plain to see,
Grave-eyed, she raised her sceptre higher
   And kindled stars upon a tree.

Then watchfires waked the sleeping marches
   Of earth and sky with flaring shout —
Back from the bounds of miracle
   Her vast compassion found us out.

We had been pent where lions raved
   And basilisks paced to and fro,

[192]

Meek now as lambs, with golden eyes
    They followed her, and we could go

Beyond the moon and waning Mars
    Behind that seraph changing-rod
Until the farthest suns grew faint
    In the excelling light of God.

TO A NUN VIOLINIST

SISTER MARY LOUISE
(*A Presentation Nun of San Francisco*)

There is a world of tenderness, within
The poignant sweetness of your violin.
There is your deepening life in Christ, that sings
Unknown to you, along the quivering strings.

There are the lilting trills of melody,
Sweet, happy sounds, that cadence joyously,
Fair, lovely dreams of songs, that seem a part
Of that true joy within the pure of heart.

And ever and anon a deeper strain
Throbs from the hidden depths a note of pain,
Of trials bravely borne, of conquered fears,
Of loneliness all God-filled through the years.

I marvel, as the vibrant, full notes flow
Into my listening heart, for now I know
The beauty of your music deep within —
Be God the Player — you, His violin.

A NUN SPEAKS TO MARY

SISTER MARY MADELEVA, C.S.C.

I

In The Days Of King Herod

You had no little maid, so I remember,
To help you sweep and tidy up the room,
To sit and watch with you that first December
Through shining twi-lights deep with golden gloom.

Through all those wistful days, you had no mother
To know your wonder and to share your joy
Of fashioning — you could not let another!
The darling swaddling garments for your Boy.

There was not any housewife to befriend you
The day word came to go to Bethlehem town;
No kinswoman bethought her to attend you
Of all the folk of David going down.

And when you held Him to your heart in wonder,
Emmanuel, God's Son, your Boy, the Word
Made flesh who shook the skies with holy thunder,
In Bethlehem not any mother stirred.

II

Sequel

Now come again the sweet Isaian days
Merciful, tender;
I know their loneliness; I dream their splendor.
Down their plain ways,
Mary, I come,
Confounded with this former shame and dumb.
Take me in service in complete surrender,
Waking and sleeping;
Take every daily task; take every duty;
Take little homely things as dusting, sweeping;
Change them into your heavenly housekeeping;
Touch them with Nazareth's most stricken beauty.
Think that my busy hands weave raiment fair
For Christ to wear;
Know that my hurrying feet
Run all your errands, Sweet;
And should they tarry,
Hear how I promise them
My Lady Mary,
That they at length may go with you to Bethlehem.
And at the last let be
On these three mute and piteous, fearful days
When none of all earth's womanfolk is near you,
That you will have to help you and to cheer you
In little foolish ways
Poor, simple me;
That when you stand outside the inn, the night wind blowing,
I will be there
Adoring, knowing;

That if the whole wide world should have no room,
I will be waiting through whatever gloom
To be your resting place. But this is heaven I dare!

So let my promise be my prayer.
And do not seek for any cave at all
With patient kine and manger crib and stall
Beyond the gates of little Bethlehem town
To lay your dear Son down.
Mother, all fair,
Lay Him within my hungry arms to sleep;
Lay Him within my hungry heart to keep,
Adorable, holy,
Little and lowly.
And let earth's shepherds, let heaven's seraphim
So find me with you Christmas night, adoring, loving him.

A QUESTION OF LOVERS

Sister Mary Madeleva, C.S.C.

There be lovers who bring me roses, the velvet of buds up-
curled;
But only one lover gives me the blossoms of all the world.

There be those who have pearls, have rubies; but much as
I care for these,
This night will my true love bring me the moon and the
Pleiedes.

I have tokens, if gifts could buy me, till love and its quest be
done.
Who will catch me a cloud's white splendor, who will fetch
me the dying sun?

Or who, on the wings of the morning, will hasten when dawn
is sweet,
To meet and possess me solely? One only with piercéd feet.

And who, for he loves me truly, will give me as token this,
This poignance of love unspoken, two wounds in his hands to
kiss?

I VISIT CARMEL

Sister Mary Madeleva, C.S.C.

Your eyes of infinite kindness meeting mine,
Your hand of quiet resting in my hand
Had been as comforting as oil and wine,
As sweet as water in a desert land.

But in this still room, hopelessly serene,
Why should I seek you, difficult and dear;
In those strange silences with peace between
How should I vainly think to find you here?

A voice as luminous and cool as dew
Is near me, though I saw not whence it came;
And you are here, sweet, inexplicable you,
Making miraculous music of my name.

Your voice, precursor in my wilderness
More blessed is, more clear than sight to me;
If there be beauty else I can not guess,
When you have healed me and when I shall see.

Only I know beatitude begun;
Only I feel no let of cloister bars,
For I have seen a splendor past the sun,
Have heard a voice beyond the listening stars.

QUESTIONS ON A NUN'S HABIT

Sister Mary Madeleva, C.S.C.

I

You do not think it is because I do not share
A woman's subtle weakness for the piquancy of dress,
Its swift, sure coquetry, its studied carelessness,
That I wear what I wear?
You do not think it is because I do not dare
Its recklessness?
What do you say
Of wearing one's bridal gown
To town,
To church on Good Friday?
Of wearing one's shroud
Every day, all day,
In the heat and the crowd
On Easter and Christmas day?
You do not tell me that I have bad taste
Or none at all, or that I am less than fastidious and proud.
Is it because you do not wish to waste
Words upon one whose world in secret you deplore?
You are not sorry for me.
You do not think me dressed quite unbecomingly?
(You would give much to be attired so adequately?)
Of all the dozen gowns I ever wore
And have abandoned, orchid, and shadow-gray and powder-
    blue,
This is the only one that you need envy me.
— You have not ever cared to find me beautiful before,
Have you?

II

Of Crowns

For captious fashion and capricious fad
I have but small concern and little care.
Not even to plait a belt for Galahad
Should I have shorn the locks that men thought fair;
But for my Lover Lord, divinely clad
I doff the shining crown that was my hair.

III

Jewelry

Pearls such as yours a proud queen quaffed one day;
A jealous queen such diamonds flung away:
Your ring once Portia might have haggled for;
Your bracelets finer are than Esther wore.
A queen brought me my beads from Nazareth,
Egypt and Judah: she was done to death
Almost in fetching them. What bitterness
She bore, from this Cross, you perhaps, may guess.
Her only Son was nailed upon it — see
Jesus of Nazareth on Calvary:
And this inscription Pilate fastened there.
Beads are the only jewelry I wear.

MARTYRS OF NAZARETH *

SISTER MARGARET MARIA
(*A Sister of Charity of Nazareth*)

Sound ye no trumpets. These
   No palms triumphant bear on high,
Silent their coming as the sweet south breeze
   Which softly treads their graves in passing by.

But Michael, hymn a song of praise,
   As nobly quiet as Nazareth;
Thy sword of battle proudly raise
   To greet the hidden martyrs' death.

No panoply, no blood-stained soil,
   No age-long honor to their name;
Engaged in charity's unselfish toil
   Death found them when he came.

Martyrs? — Ah yes! They went forth, calm, to greet,
   As though a friend, the cholera's grim touch,
Counting love's service to his victims sweet,
   Nor thought, if death the price, they paid too much.

* The cholera scourged the country in 1832-33. The Sisters of Charity
of Nazareth closed their schools and nursed the sick. Two lost their
lives in this labor of love, and were probably the first religious women in
the United States to die in the service of their countrymen. During the
yellow fever and smallpox epidemics they nursed the sick and several
died martyrs to duty.

Many nursed the soldiers during the Civil War, and one was killed
near the battle line. In 1858 the grateful citizens of Holly Springs, Miss.,
erected a monument to the six sisters who had died there during the
scourge.   *Editor's Note*

Thus two of them won heaven. Close behind
    Come yellow fever's victims, unafraid
In its contagious deadliness to find
    An open gate and enter undismayed.

Yet others small-pox dare, its hideous mien
    Revealing to their eyes, by faith made clear
A hidden beauty to all else unseen —
    They see a light where all is dark with fear.

And some amidst war's hate-beclouded air
    With love for all attend the battle's prey,
Nor do they shrink when one is called to share
    With earlier martyrs heaven's eternal day.

Yet braver they who once in vision bright
    Saw glory gleaming through the gates ajar,
And, stricken by pain's sword, yet living, fight
    O'er rocky pathways to the goal afar.

IN MEMORY OF
MOTHER SERAPHINE IRELAND *

SISTER MARIS STELLA
(*A Sister of St. Joseph of St. Paul, Minn.*)

Spoil not her rest by singing threnodies.
Let her sleep now. Light tapers by the bed,
Fold the fine hands at last — now she is dead.
Little there is to do now that can please
The tired body, since those enemies
Of life — sickness and age — bowed down the head
Still valiant till the last brave word was said,
The last articulate fiat. Elegies
Would be for such a one as futile now
As waters cast upon the ample wave,
Her soul would deprecate those filial pains,
Compassionate for our folly, knowing how
We see but darkly still this side the grave.
Let prayers be said. Her soul with God remains.

* Mother Seraphine was a Sister of Saint Joseph. Her brother was Archbishop Ireland of St. Paul, Minnesota.

Editor's Note

A NUN'S HOBBY

SISTER MARY OF THE ANGELS
(*A Sister of Mercy of Chicago*)

I have a little hobby of saving odds and ends
To fashion into trinkets for near and distant friends.

The ribbon from the candy box, nice paper in designs,
The linings of gay envelopes, and cards, and valentines.

Some clever words from current ads and cryptic epigrams
To slip into a little note or even telegrams.

Each day brings some occasion for ingenuity
In putting them together in magic harmony.

Thus something comes from nothing and much from little
    grows,
The rapture of creation which every artist knows!

From little odds and ends of life I fashion beauty too
And find a wealth of loveliness in everything I do.

I gather crumbs from tables where geniuses are fed
And the star-dust of creation becomes my daily bread.

PROFESSION SONG
"A Bundle of Myrrh Is My Beloved"

SISTER MARY OF THE VISITATION
(*A Visitation Nun of Catonsville, Md.*)

He that is Joy through meadows of joyance hath led me —
He that is Sweet
Hath with the sweetness of infinite sweetness fed me;
Gives me to eat
Of the fruits of His bounty, delighting my soul's long desir-
      ings —
Lays at my feet
All that my heart, with its longings and ceaseless aspirings,
Hastens to meet.
He that is fair with infinite Beauty hath wooed me —
He that is fair —
For He dwells in stars of the heavens, in flowers of the field,
In birds of the air;
And I know that the white souls of children unceasingly give
      Him
Their exquisite prayer.
He that is fair with infinite Beauty hath wooed me —
He that is fair.

But He that is Love, ah, with infinite Sorrow hath won me—
Dieth for me.
"See how my soul (since that Thou hast so sweetly undone
      me)
Flieth to Thee."
"Like unto myrrh?" Ah, but sweeter than sweetness and lovely
All beauty above!
He that is Love with infinite Sorrow hath won me —
He that is Love.

[206]

A CARMELITE BREAKS SILENCE
"We are heaven." St. Augustine

SISTER MIRIAM
(*A Sister of Mercy of Dallas, Penn.*)

God's house is heaven and it is here within
   My breast, invaded by the Three. No need
   Have I the world I left, to wander in,
   To follow foolishly where false roads lead:
No need to scan the multitudinous words
Men use to hide or to uncover Him.
   Love is enough, now clear as psalms of birds
   The mysteries are that tease the seraphim.

THE TOWER OF LOWLINESS
For a Maryknoll Nun

SISTER MIRIAM
(*A Sister of Mercy of Dallas, Penn.*)

Lady, scholar, poet, saint, you ask
Where lies a steeper way to climb the tower
Of lowliness. With unconcern you mask
Your sanctity, your sanctifying power.

Where you have fared how few aspire or care
To walk. Men love the petalled path that leads
To where you never are; refuse to share
The hazard of the road your spirit needs.

Not Beatrice herself in subtler ways,
Flushed by the reddening of unseen lips,
Stirred mortal man immortal God to praise
On earth in a divine apocalypse.

So long you contemplated God in prayer
I search your face to find His mirrored there.

VICTIM INVISIBLE*
*For Mother M. Carmelita, Founder of The Sisters of
Mercy of the Union in the United States*

SISTER MIRIAM
(*A Sister of Mercy of Dallas, Penn.*)

No corpus hangs upon the cross I wear,
  No broken hands and feet, no thorn-torn head;
  The ebony and ivory are bare
Of evidence that any blood was shed.

Well fed, well clothed, well shod, and housed as well,
  Can I invisibly the victim be,
Unless in mind and heart I daily dwell
  In spirit with Him on the bitter tree?

* Hanging from the rosary the Sisters of Mercy wear is an ebony cross
inlaid with one of ivory and without the image of the dead body of Our
Lord.

Editor's Note

THE REPLY

Sister Monica
(*An Ursuline Nun of Brown County, Ohio*)

Voice of the World:
>"Your feet tread no rhythms of the dance!
>You walk demure to your door!"

The Nun:
>"But many a little child dances for me
>   On the gold of Heaven's floor!
>And my dearth shall enrich and emancipate
>   Through ages to come as of yore."

The World:
>"No comrades drink to your health
>In your silent refectory!"

The Nun:
>"But my name is toast at the joyous board
>   Where John makes minstrelsy.
>I am the ringing pledge of man's
>   Final self-mastery."

The World:
>"No lovers knock at your gate
>As you fasten your long black veil."

The Nun:
>"But there is a path all white with the Feet
>   Of One I know Who is sweet, sweet,

Whose strength makes all life hale;
And I breathe the hope to a yearning world
   That spirit at last will prevail."

The World:
      "You have no husband to toil
      With his hands for your love and your stay."

The Nun:
      "But the deathless Joy Who gave Adam Eve
         Is weaving for me all day.
      I light the torch for the marriage-bond
         To follow up heights I essay!"

The World:
      "The child at your knee is not yours,
      Whom you teach from your thumb-worn book."

The Nun:
      "Oh my forehead shall glow with a radiance spun
         By angels of children foregone!
      For I am the mother of mothers to be
         Through my spirit-travail of chastity;
      The dreaming Race, unaware, looks to me
         Where I move with my face to the dawn."

THE TEACHER*

Sister Monica

I

This School: like larks, in the clod low down
In the hedge aloof, when the wind is strong —
Oh here is mothering for me:
   For here is cradle and here is song
   Of struggling, fluttering, nesting birds,
   Warm, tender little breasts, and new
Wings of down that beat their way swift flying to the blue.

II

Why here is the very purple of power.
Here hangs my star with its radiance mild:
And the light of my star shall never set
Who minister unto the soul of a child.
   Let all the monster masses forge the old earth's future
   As they can;
But I am rich in the plastic power
That shapes the race of man.

III

I watch my birds as they soar and soar;
   I hear their silver melody.
In wing and music I catch the pulse
   Of the life that was once in me.
Mine is the flight and mine the song
   As they float on the wind's keen edge:
Mine: who plumed and tuned and fired
   In the nest aloof in the hedge.

* To my mind, of course, as an Ursuline, "The Teacher" really means
the Ursuline.

Author's Note

[212]

IV

They beat their eager wings in my face
As they mount and hover and soar again;
They buffet me with storms of cries
Breaking to rhapsody's tender rain.
   They lash me with young anger's thong, and the scorn
      of life
   That is born anew;
But their eye catches flame from the spark in mine
   And off they go to the blue!

HIDE AND SEEK

SISTER MARY PHILIP, C.S.C.

I sweep the cloisters
   Long and dim,
Thinking of the
   Seraphim.

Faint, in sooth, need
   Be the guise
To hide them from
   My feeble eyes.

Fainter, still, the
   Guise of One
Who daily walks here,
   Mary's Son.

Finding Him, in truth
   Were sweet,
But hid His nail-pierced
   Hands and feet —

Hid with all a
   Master's art
And foolish, I, and
   Slow of heart

To see in each who
   Goes this way
But Christ, and so
   Find Him to-day.

Dull am I, and
　　Passing weak
At playing Heavenly
　　Hide and Seek.

'Tis so I sweep the
　　Cloisters dim,
Thinking on the
　　Seraphim.

SAINT TERESA OF AVILA
(*A Carmelite Nun*)

SISTER MARY SAINT VIRGINIA, B.V.M.

I feel towards you as toward a meagre few
Who down this earth have walked and breathed this air.
Not that you mothered souls do I hold you
The one of women who defies compare
(Save one, a Lily blown from Galilee)—
Not that you taught and teach the learnéd of
The lore of laughter and the theory,
The metaphysics, and the art of love —
Woman of fire, flaming through challenged cell,
Not even that your light outlines Him best: —
But that at once you held the citadel
And held my lonely Love against your breast;
But that you walked in streets, yet walked apart
And let Him warm His dear hands at your heart.

ARCUM CONTERET
(*For a Nun Violinist*)

Sister Mary Thérèse, Sor. D. S.

The dusk is sudden with luminous music flooding
The white, cool cloisters glowing as Aaron's rod
With radiance of living lilies budding
Beautiful with God.
In low, sweet surging of song through the hush come stealing
Motifs Brunhilda and Iseult had bartered for dole;
Music that bruises, that shatters with marvelous healing
The God-vibrant soul.
Is it the wild cry of a heart to unburden its treasure,
Or rapturous plaint of a joy-stricken soul that sings?
A heart is poised with a bow, its loving to measure
In sobbings of tremulous strings.
And the message it tells in this hour of ineffable dreaming,
For aeons eternal in God's burning bosom has lain —
The heart's bitter cry is not futile, nor hopelessly seeming
Nor uttered in vain.
For with undaunted aim while this most brief life still lingers,
Song arrows shall rend the impervious heavens apart —
Till her Lover, defenceless, shall strike the frail bow from her
fingers,
Catching her to His heart.

CHRISTMAS IN CARMEL*
(*For the nuns of the Carmel of the Mother of God*)

SISTER MARY THÉRÈSE, SOR. D. S.

Now in this quiet love-illumined night
My wistful soul will be a Carmelite

And at the grill within the holy place,
Bend low to gaze upon a Child's small face.

In the blue midnight, underneath the sky,
All of my suppliant soul melts in a cry —

Kindle me with some white Teresian flame,
Who wear the subtle wonder of her name,

That in the marts of men I walk apart
Keeping a cloistered and untroubled heart.

And give me of the gentle Doctor's fire
Who wooed the cross and died of its desire,

That up bright Carmel's mountain I be led,
On crumbs of mystic wisdom comforted.

Then fold within your Hands, secure and whole,
The precious loves You knit into my soul.

With this small lifted song my heart I bring
Here to your Carmel cradle, little King.

---

* This poem was written at the request of the late Mother Paula of the
Mother of God, D. C., Foundress of the Milwaukee Carmel, and was
sung by the Carmelites at their crib after Midnight Mass, December
25, 1940.

Author's Note

[218]

ON A FAVORITE POET
(*Sister Mary Madeleva, C. S. C.*)

SISTER MARY THÉRÈSE, SOR. D. S.

Exquisite reaper in a field of song.
Athwart the crimson dawn I see you stand,
Your golden sheaves of singing in your hand,
Caroling myriad melodies that throng
Your soul's white cloister, and your lips make sweet —
Sweeter than breath of rose and asphodel.
Why have you caught my spirit in your spell,
That I should strew my singing at your feet?

There is an effluence from God's dear face,
Kindles your rapture with a winsome grace;
Song-miracles of sweet-panged anguish wrought
Halo the virgin love-towers of your thought —
Whence to my heart this peace no tumult quells,
Whence to my soul this silver peal of bells.

PORT-OF-CALL
(*Passing Spain, September 1939*)

Sister Mary Thérèse, Sor. D. S.

A quiver of wings and the gulls dip into the sunset,
My heart leans with them to starboard eagerly
As spectral and stark the sierras of Andalusia
Rise from a sun-flecked sea.

We pause at no port for the seas are sown with peril;
We shall trail the dark through the pillars of Hercules;
But the human soul may leap the waves unfettered
Of such contingencies

To this land of the Moor, the mystic, the bright-robed martyr,
Of John the seraphic, whose soul was a lonely flame;
But my heart cries out to that greatest of all her women
A thousand Carmels' name.

I walk the streets still sweet with the press of her sandals,
The winding paths that re-echo the petulant beat
Of her mule's small hoofs, as Teresa rode into the morning
In the wake of the Paraclete.

I kneel at her side by the little grated window
And feel the hot pulse of her prayer, the divine instress
Of a love that she followed with passionate, wild abandon
Through streets of bitterness.

I thrill at the words that have told me of all her doctrine
Of what rich fibre her soul, how sternly true —

"Will I open the grill? O Gratian, how little you know me!
I would open my heart to you!"

The shoreline drops within God's bluest ocean;
There are tears on my cheek, and the sky is a misty pall
Where only the silver track of a gull marks eastward
The spirit's port-of-call.

TO A NUN-STIGMATIST

SISTER MARY THÉRÈSE, SOR. D.S.

My hands within your hand;
My fingers touch a scar
Etched keener than the night
Cut by the sharpest star.

We spoke of simple things
Meant for the lips alone:
Far lands that I had seen,
Quaint nuns that you had known.

Yet deep beneath our words
Like song lost in a wood
Your heart cried out to mine,
My spirit understood.

Soul-fibre seared to ash;
Heart bruised and desolate;
This is the secret pact
Of the initiate.

Since on the mystic tree
Blossomed the twisted thorn
By every several branch
This token must be worn.

There is divine intent
In every wounding thing
That holds the heart elate,
That makes the spirit sing.

THE NUN'S VOW

SISTER MARY WILFRID
(*A Sister of Loretto of Kentucky*)

O Lord, dear Lord, behold me at Thy feet,
While years are few and life appeareth sweet,
Yet conscious that the shining world can give
Nor joy, nor treasure, that fore'er shall live.
No lowering shadows hath my path o'erspread,
No dark forboding yet awakened dread;
The vistas of the future seemeth bright,
And still my heart desires a holier light.

I want Thee, Lord. No creature else can fill
The inner void; no other voice can thrill,
In low-toned music, floating on white waves,
As when the sea, a sun-parched shore line bathes.
It might have brought content, at least in part,
To rest mine own upon another heart,
And quaff sweet draughts of human love, all pure,
Save for the thought — how long will this endure?

Thus grew the yearning for some higher prize,
Some pledge of love and hope that never dies,
A bond secure, unfailing as Thy word;
None such could give, save only Thee, dear Lord.
The voice of pleasure chanted in the vale,
The song of triumph echoed on the gale,
Domestic joys in willing accents called,
But none of these reclaimed a soul once thralled

By chains of Thine. The weakness, sin and woe,
Thou foundest in me, did not my claim forego,
With all the misery, a hope was there;
I turned to Thee; Thou didst not spurn my prayer.
Gladness this hour doth in my heart hold sway,
I'm Thine, dear Lord, and will be Thine alway:
Oh! that my words could summon to Thy shrine,
Young hearts, more fervent, purer far than mine!

My chains are golden with a clasp empearled,
They guard me from a cold and dangerous world,
Each link is welded by the Hand Of Love,
Annealed to strength by seraph flames above.
I feel protection in each lightsome bond,
And tender care, and peace, all else beyond;
Content am I, Thy gracious will allows,
My lips to speak, to-day, my holy vows.